C000072540

JOHN HORNE TOOKE Esqr

From a contemporary engraving in the Department of Prints and Drawings of the
British Museum

THE PRISON DIARY
(16 May–22 November 1794)
OF
JOHN HORNE TOOKE

edited with introduction and notes by

A. V. BEEDELL and A. D. HARVEY

LEEDS
THE LEEDS PHILOSOPHICAL AND LITERARY SOCIETY LTD
November 1995

Proceedings of the Leeds Philosophical and Literary Society, Literary and Historical Section, Vol. XXIV, Part III, pp. 133–262.

The Leeds Philosophical and Literary Society Ltd.,

City Museum,

Calverley Street,

Leeds LS1 3AA

Editor, Literary and Historical Section

IAN MOXON, M.A.

University of Leeds

British Library Cataloguing-in-Publication Data:
a catalogue record for this book is available from the British Library.

ISBN 1-870737-08-3

Printed in Great Britain by Stephen Austin and Sons Ltd., Hertford

CONTENTS

INTRODUCTION

In one of the most contentious and sensational criminal prosecutions ever mounted by the British state against private individuals, the veteran reformer John Horne Tooke was one of eight men who found themselves imprisoned in the Tower of London pending trial for high treason in 1794. Before presenting the diary which he kept during the twenty-seven weeks and two days of his imprisonment, it seems appropriate to explain something of the background to his arrest and prosecution.

There can be little doubt that by the spring of 1794 there was genuine anxiety not only in government, but also in some opposition circles, concerning the security of the British Isles. The disappointing performance of British and allied armies on the Continent against revolutionary France was only part of the problem. Equally disturbing were the prospect of internal disaffection and alleged evidence of political subversion by organizations thought to be ready to aid a French invasion and form an alternative, revolutionary, government in England. Had the conduct of the war been more successful, such fears might have been swept aside; but from the commencement of hostilities in February 1793 there had been little to celebrate. Not until 1 June 1794 did Howe win his naval victory, and the decisive land victory, so looked for, had not materialized. The fear of internal subversion and insurrection was amplified, however, by other, tangential, factors.

Two and a half decades of effort by extra-parliamentary groups to deconstruct the ruling oligarchy via a campaign for parliamentary reform — a campaign to which Pitt, even as prime minister, had once contributed — had not been totally without effect in educating public opinion. There was also the increasingly volatile and hostile response of some sections of the population to altered economic relationships between labour, wages, and subsistence in favour of capital — a growing sense of alienation reflected, if not in any particular increase in mob activity (a fact of life in eighteenth-century Britain in any case), then in the rising incidence of crime, in criticism of the harshness of the law in regard to crimes against property, and in the increasingly high profile of working people generally. What the French Revolution suddenly offered was the very real possibility that these two elements — genteel parliamentary reformers on the one hand and what Burke called the 'swinish multitude' on the other — would come together to overthrow the British state. Pitt certainly understood this. He accused the political societies of hiding behind a mask of reform while all the time stirring up the resentments of workers in the manufacturing towns, 'ignorant and profligate men', in a planned conspiracy to overthrow 'Government, law, property, security, religion, order and every thing valuable in this country as they had already overturned and destroyed every thing in France'. An 'enormous torrent of insurrection', in his view, was being planned by the despicable and contemptible leaders of the London Corresponding Society (henceforth LCS), whose capacity to extend its own numbers Pitt described as 'unbounded'. Pitt, seeking leave to bring in a bill to suspend Habeas Corpus, made this famous speech on the day that Horne Tooke was arrested, 16 May 1794.[1]

The torrent of Pitt's denunciation of the reformers had its fount, of course, in the emotional rhetoric of the ex-Whig Edmund Burke, whose *Reflections on the Revolution in France* of 1790 had articulated all the deep, irrational terrors felt by the establishment at the idea of change *per se*. Indeed, the ideological watershed of the French Revolution had made the difference between Whig opposition and the government almost irrelevant, as the July 1794 junction of the Portland Whigs with the government side demonstrated. What seemed to be at issue was not simply Pitt's government, but survival or annihilation of an entire culture, the culture of the English ruling élite and with it all its assumptions about the way the world was made — assumptions which declared all order and civilization to be inextricably bound up with the aristo-cratic ideal of landed, inherited privilege supported by religion, law, and the constitution.

But, on a more simple, gut level, what was at stake was the control of the British state by an entrenched power group, represented in most of its facets, from plebeian outsider to aristocratic grandee, by the chief actors directly involved in the repression: not only Pitt, but his lord chancellor, Loughborough (an ex-reformer), his attorney general, Sir John Scott (later Lord Eldon, a Tory's Tory of humble Newcastle origin), his home secretary till July 1794, the bluff, affably savage Scotsman, Henry Dundas (known in Scotland by the sobriquet 'Harry the Ninth'), and, after July, the patrician Portland. Beneath them, but equally committed to sustaining the status quo, were the placemen: notably Evan Nepean, the under-secretary to the Home Department; Joseph White, the treasury solicitor, and John Reeves, former colonial judge and founder of the patriotic associations movement, whose love of his king was only equalled by his love of government office. As he himself put it, when he was appealing to Windham for assistance in his fight for the patent of king's printer in August 1794:

The misfortune is, that we are all too apt to think much of ourselves under two sorts of circumstances — One is where we are too much neglected; the other where we want to make something of ourselves — Both these apply to me — I declare the former with some resentment, and I confess the latter with great frankness, or unworthy selfishness. I have given up myself, for several years, to objects of a public nature [the associations movement], while others have been pursuing lucrative employments and I have finally attached myself to the King's government, in an official connexion, by which all my prospects in life are to be determined.

There was no way of getting forward, he said, 'but by the notice of the govern-ment; and if I am disappointed in that quarter, it is like another man being thwarted in his private vocation & employment'.[2] In those days men were not embarrassed to confess to a vested interest.

The conscious, active, resistance to the assumptions of the ruling élite (and of those who, like Reeves and others, were dependent upon it) by dissenters contesting the Test and Corporation acts and by middle-class elements protesting about their own continued social irrelevance and political impotence had been at the very heart of British politics for over twenty years. That the outcome had not been resolved, that the sides were not all that clearly defined, and that the contest was even temporarily lost sight of when the events of 1789 in France burst upon Europe complicated an already complex situation, in which the curious ambivalence of Pitt himself was an enduring element. The action of Pitt and his ministry in striking at the extra-parliamentary reform societies, the intellectual, if largely ineffectual, cutting-edge of resistance to patrician assumptions — and in so doing at a figure like John Horne Tooke (once a supporter of Pitt) — has to be seen in this rather muddled context.

From 1780 the most prestigious and influential of these societies had been the London-based Society for Constitutional Information (henceforth SCI), closely associated with Dr. John Jebb, Major John Cartwright, and later John Horne Tooke. With a strong flavour of dissent, it was nevertheless a distinctly polite society, which from time to time attracted men of stature and influence such as the dukes of Norfolk and Richmond, Richard Brinsley Sheridan, and Philip Francis. The aims of the society — the reform of the basis of parliamentary representation (at that time effectively controlled in parliament by a relatively small number of peers in the House of Lords, and outside parliament by a clique of wealthy families) and the curbing of the powers of patronage of the crown — had never been perceived as revolutionary, not least because of its genteel membership; nor, by the advent of the revolution in France, was the society regarded as a significant political factor, in view of the decline in its activity. This decline was largely due to the failure of Pitt by 1785, even as prime minister, to get his reforming legislation through parliament, and to the predictable schisms within the SCI itself which had surrounded the attempt.[3] But in the wake of the revolution in France came a new burst of energy and enthusiasm. The society, reduced to intimate meetings at the home of its secretary, Daniel Adams, became once more a viable (if less select) organization with regular public meetings at the Crown and Anchor tavern just off the Strand.[4]

The SCI, although boasting dukes in its membership, was very largely composed of respectable men of commerce and the professions who, on one level, embedded their political and social disaffection in the cultural matrix of Graeco-Roman Enlightenment ideals of efficiency, civic purity, and personal stoicism, and, on another level, in the supposed philosophy of 1688, namely, the rights of freeborn Protestant Englishmen, balanced against the rights of the landed aristocracy and the limited prerogatives of the crown, in support of one overriding principle — the protection of private property. In no way could their rhetoric thus be construed as revolutionary. They could have had no truck with thinkers like Thomas Spence, whose communistic views on property were, for such men, akin to lunacy. Nor on the whole could they, with comfort, accommodate the outright republicanism of Thomas Paine, certainly not those of them, like Horne Tooke, who were on the episcopalian rather than on the dissenting side of the Protestant sectarian divide. Indeed, most felt happiest on the safe intellectual and moral ground of 1688, vigilantly guarding the sacred and inalienable rights of Englishmen against the encroachments of the crown; against the corrupting power of patronage; against a corrupt oligarchic Whig aristocracy. They were content, then, to see the problem as historical rather than ideological — as a question of mere conservation of what was perceived, essentially, to be a near-perfect instrument of government — the 1688 British constitution.[5] (And in this, of course, ironically, they were not far removed from the position of the Foxite Whig opposition or from that of the 1792 Society of the Friends of the People, formed by the younger Whigs to shift the leadership of the reform movement from plebeian to patrician hands.) Such a shallow, mechanistic analysis as that of the SCI barely hid the depth and bitterness of its members' class resentment, kept in check by the need to remain firmly inside the social parameters set by the demands of respectable conformity. Nor should it be imagined that the inadequacy of their philosophical arguments, indeed, the virtual absence of a sophisticated ideology with which to mediate their real position *vis-à-vis* the state, made them any less certain of their intrinsic moral and intellectual superiority over their aristocratic foes. Yet, by their need for social acceptability they were, in effect, tied in to the very pattern they wished to alter, if not destroy.

Nevertheless, by the end of 1791 the SCI was making an important niche for itself as the model for a new burgeoning of constitutional societies around the country, maintaining a nurturing correspondence with them but at the same time being drawn into deeper and more dangerous political waters. It was through such networks that the SCI distributed part I of Paine's *The Rights of Man.*

The LCS, founded in 1792, was a very different proposition — a working men's association, dedicated to the duke of Richmond's scheme of 1780 for annual parliaments and universal suffrage but less interested in historically based rights apropos of 1688 (although it publicly espoused them as did even Paine on occasion), and increasingly interested in the radical Painite principle of the natural rights of all men, which discarded the aristocracy, the monarchy, and even 1688, as guardians of individual freedom. Branches (divisions) were formed all over London and links were forged with societies in major industrial centres, especially Manchester, Sheffield, and Norwich, and with the SCI as well. And it was this linking of the old and once respectable issues in the shape of the SCI with what were perceived to be the new revolutionary and decidedly disreputable principles of the LCS that so disturbed the authorities.

There had been much to-ing and fro-ing across the Channel on the part of members of the societies, and other prominent people — Lord Daer, Priestley, Frost, Paine, Muir, Felix Vaughan, Cooper, Henry Redhead Yorke, and others — who not only visited France but mixed with French revolutionary politicians.[6] On 14 July 1790, 650 people met for a grand dinner (held under the auspices of the SCI and presided over by Lord Stanhope) at the Crown and Anchor just off the Strand to celebrate the first anniversary of the fall of the Bastille. Sheridan moved

That this meeting does most cordially rejoice in the establishment and confirmation of liberty in France, and that it beholds, with peculiar satisfaction, the sentiments of amity and good will which appear to pervade the people of that country towards this kingdom, especially at a time when it is the manifest interest of both states that nothing should interrupt the harmony that at present subsists between them, and which is so essential for the freedom and happiness, not only of both nations, but of all mankind.

Horne Tooke, in a move typical both of his political ambivalence as well as of the legal pedantry which was later to help save him from the gallows, surprised and angered many when he suggested the following amendment, which, when resisted, he proposed and carried as a separate resolution:

We feel equal satisfaction that the subjects of England, by the virtuous exertions of their ancestors, have not so arduous a task to perform as the French had; but have only to maintain and improve the constitution, which their forefathers have transmitted to them.[7a]

Sheridan as a member of parliament was, of course, less vulnerable to prosecution than a private citizen, which may have been the thinking behind Horne Tooke's amendment. Possibly though, it was simply Horne Tooke's method of maintaining his own personal position as distinct from that of the Whigs, with whom he had long been politically unfriendly. Nevertheless there were many shared attitudes and opinions between Sheridan and Horne Tooke which were later to be reinforced by the dedicated opposition of each to the war.

Up until the commencement of hostilities in February 1793, public statements continued to be made in support of the French and their revolution. In November 1792 John Frost, an attorney and prominent member of the SCI, with Joel Barlow, the American writer and politician, presented to the national convention in France an address from the SCI congratulating them 'upon the triumphs of liberty'.[7b] It did not go unnoticed by a British government alarmed at developments abroad and threatened by signs of disorder, discontent, and subversion at home. Frost was prosecuted on a trumped-up charge of seditious words the following year, found guilty, and sentenced to imprisonment for six months, to exposure in the pillory, and to be struck off the roll of attorneys. It was only a matter of time before an anxious administration, galvanized by the spectre of French Jacobinism, used its authority even more emphatically and with greater system. Indeed the first public intimation of government unease had come in the proclamation of 21 May 1792 against seditious meetings and writings. According to the (admittedly rather coloured) recollection of Thomas Holcroft, this had already unleashed a wave of hysteria and repression in the provinces:

Prosecutions were immediately commenced throughout the kingdom. Every county assize and quarter sessions condemned some poor ignorant enthusiast to imprisonment . . . and men of respectable characters and honest intentions, in the fury of their new-born zeal, thought it a heroical act of duty to watch the conduct of their very intimates.[8]

Holcroft, a close friend of William Godwin, and a man who believed passionately in the power of facts — in the enlightening power of reason — whatever his theatrical overstatement, was quite evidently shocked at the sudden alteration of the social and political climate.

Future ages will find it difficult to believe that Government through its agents, could condescend to use the means which were resorted to, that this spirit might be kept alive; and that the hatred already generated between friends, families, societies and sects, might continue and increase. Many of its partisans openly affirmed it was desirable that the contest should be brought to an issue;[9]

For Holcroft, the son of an itinerant cobbler, reason was not only his human birthright but also the justification of his social ambition. Reason was a moral force in its own right, which, in the absence of a more refined ideology, justified the political claims of the entire middle class to which he now belonged. The whole progress of the eighteenth-century Graeco-Roman Enlightenment for Holcroft and most bourgeois intellectuals had been nothing if not a promise of continuous human improvement under the aegis of reason. The ultimate perfectibility of human nature had seemed no utopian dream, and the French Revolution no more than another inevitable step along the way —the throwing-off of papist superstition and the embracing of pure reason as a guiding principle of action.

It is not surprising then that Holcroft should have been so shocked to see his dream swept aside in a brutal reassertion of the old interest-based prejudices. He describes the initial response of the SCI to the wave of government-sponsored anti-Jacobin hysteria as one of 'amazement' and 'stupefaction'. These men, like Dr. Richard Brocklesby, James Parkinson, James Mackintosh, John Horne Tooke, John Cartwright, all at one time members of the SCI, and others such as Joseph Priestley, Erasmus Darwin, Thomas Beddoes, and William Godwin, had believed themselves in the intellectual vanguard of the nation. They had taken for granted that thinking men since the time of Locke ultimately agreed with their basic position. They knew that the prime minister himself did. Suddenly the aegis of reason had become an accusation. Suddenly, as Holcroft said, 'Each man saw himself the butt of obloquy'. And immediately above their heads, upstairs at the Crown and Anchor tavern, the personification of this obloquy, John Reeves and his Association for the Preservation of Liberty and Property against Republicans and Levellers, was from November 1792 'a focus of the opprobrium cast on them all'.[10] They had no satisfactory answer to this sudden alteration in their position, especially since the government was using their own political arguments as evidence against them. The establishment was to be highly successful in mobilizing 1688, the crown, the constitution, and the defence of property as the pivotal elements of its propaganda war against the societies—epitomized in the activities of Reeves's association and its hundreds (possibly thousands) of spiritual clones that sprang up around the country, or at least were supposed to have sprung up.[11]

The response of many in the SCI was to withdraw altogether. The response of others, however, was towards greater militancy and greater contact with more extreme groups — like the LCS. There can be little doubt that this latter course was the one followed by Horne Tooke and his closest associates in the SCI, not because he was a Painite, an accusation he denied to the very end of his life, but arguably because the depth of his sense of social and political antagonism had led him into a position of habitual confrontation with the ruling élite from which he could not withdraw. He was a man, it was said at least by his enemies, who was never content without a grievance. On the other hand it would not be altogether fanciful to hypothesize that he saw in the growing storm a last chance for grasping real political power. He was nearly sixty and had reaped up till then no rewards for his lifelong political activism. Writing in the ultra-Tory *Blackwood's Edinburgh Magazine* in 1833, George Croly, in a retrospective and highly prejudiced analysis of Horne Tooke (seen as the archetype of an evil democrat), nevertheless sums up Horne Tooke's position in 1792 rather well.

After this lesson of the inconveniences of rabble ambition [his 1790 contest for Westminster against Fox and his failure in 1792 successfully to defend himself in Fox's ensuing action for debt], Horne Tooke retired from London for life. He gave up a house which he had in Richmond Buildings, Soho, for the purpose of concentrating his pursuits or his partisans, and fixed himself finally at Wimbledon. By what pecuniary resources this change was accomplished, it is not now easy to discover. He had long since exhausted his apparent means; his trade of public life had been signally unprosperous; fine and imprisonment, law and damages, were the only fruits which he had gleaned from the field of politics: disowned by party, discountenanced by Ministers, trampled down in the triumph of the Whig elections, despised and repelled by the Tories, and rejected even by the rabble, no man could have had stronger reasons for hiding his diminished head, shrinking from the society in which he could find no place, and giving up the rest of his days to the obscurity, which, in such men, is the only retreat from public ridicule.[12]

After all, nobody could have foreseen then the ultimate triumph of Pitt — eventually to be apotheosized as the saving spirit of the English nation. Horne Tooke could be forgiven for thinking that his last chance for victory had come riding in on the back of the French Revolution.

The impetus which led the government almost inexorably towards the use of judicial terror in the suppression of political dissent had already begun, as we have seen, with the proclamation of May 1792. It gathered pace in Scotland in late 1793 and early 1794, with the break-up of the Scottish and British conventions in Edinburgh[13] and the savage sentencing by the Scottish courts of its leaders: Muir, Skirving, Gerrald, and Margarot (fourteen years transportation each), and Fyshe Palmer (seven years transportation). There was an outcry from London and motions were put to parliament[14] condemning the trials of Muir and Fyshe Palmer as illegal, partly on the grounds that Robert McQueen Lord Braxfield, the lord justice clerk, had conducted the trials with outrageously crude partiality and a hand-picked jury. There was much public sympathy, especially in the societies, and fear was even expressed that Dundas was planning to deport reformers to Scotland in order to get convictions which would not be possible under English law.

In London, on 20 January 1794, at a packed meeting of the LCS at the Globe tavern in Fleet Street, John Martin delivered an inflammatory speech which called upon Englishmen to choose between liberty and slavery, and to make preparations for a general convention of the people 'upon the first introduction [by parliament] of any bill, or motion, inimical to the liberties of the people'.[15a] The SCI resolved at its meeting of the 24 January that 'the London Corresponding Society have deserved well of their country' and that 40,000 copies of Martin's speech should be printed.[15b] The treasury solicitor, Joseph White, on 11 April sent on twenty-one alarming reports of meetings to Dundas.[16] On 14 April at a mass meeting at Chalk Farm the LCS passed resolutions backing the formation of a national convention in London. The meeting was attended by government spies. There was also a report current at that time of the French being about to invade; this had been circulated by the garrulous William Stone on the authority of his brother John Hurford Stone, who was in Paris, and were made sinister by the involvement of William Jackson, who, with Stone, was later to be tried for high treason. This led to a series of interrogations by the Privy Council and the embarrassing involvement of several prominent Whig politicians including Lord Lauderdale, Sheridan, and Benjamin Vaughan. In examining Vaughan, the Privy Council had thought fit to ask whether Jackson (in the government's sights for some time), en route to Ireland, had had contact in England with Priestley or with Horne Tooke. Vaughan's negative response may not have convinced the Privy Council. Indeed, the Second Report from the Committee of Secrecy to the House of Commons on 6 June made a special point of associating the SCI with this affair.[17] On 2 May at a rowdy SCI dinner at the Crown and Anchor republican toasts were drunk, 'Ça Ira' and the 'Marseillaise' were sung, and Horne Tooke stood up and denounced the parliament as a 'scoundrel sink of corruption'.[18]

On 12 May 1794, in spite of legal opinion that was less than confident of the government's ability to mount a case under English law, the arrests in London began: chiefly of the leaders and members of the LCS and the SCI including, by the 14th, Thomas Hardy the secretary and founder of the LCS, John Thelwall, and the Revd. Jeremiah Joyce. Before his arrest, Joyce had written to

Horne Tooke the following letter, which the latter assumed to have been the cause of his own arrest.

DEAR CITIZEN

This morning at six o'clock, Citizen Hardy was taken away by an order from the Secretary of State's office, they seized every thing they could lay hands on — Query — Is it possible to get ready by Thursday?

Yours,

J. Joyce

It had been intercepted, and the government, according to Horne Tooke, had presumed that the question 'Is it possible to get ready by Thursday?' referred to a planned insurrection. Later in open court Horne Tooke forced the prosecution to produce the letter and was able to prove that Joyce's question referred only to the proposed publication of a list, taken from the court calendar, of places and pensions enjoyed by Mr. Pitt and his family.[19]

But Horne Tooke's assumption was probably incorrect, since he had been under suspicion for some time and was thought by the government to be one of those planning a national convention (see below). In any case, he was duly arrested on 16 May and brought before the Privy Council for questioning, before being committed to the Tower to await trial. Seven others were also committed to the Tower on charges of high treason: Thomas Hardy, John Thelwall, the Revd. Jeremiah Joyce, John Augustus Bonney, John Richter, Stewart Kyd, and John Lovett. A further five were eventually named on the same indictment: Thomas Holcroft, Mathew Moore, Thomas Wardle, Richard Hodgson, and John Baxter. It is these thirteen men who are generally supposed to be the subjects of this particular judicial action; but, out of at least forty persons rounded up at that time, there were several others who were charged with high treason, though not on the same indictment: John Martin, John Philip Francklow, John Ashley, John Hillier, Thomas Spence, John Roussell, as well as the Pop-gun Plot suspects (see p. 13), Paul Thomas Lemaitre, George Higgins, and John Smith, who were arrested in late September.[20]

It is possible to argue that it had been the volatile situation in Scotland in 1792/1793 which had triggered off the repression in London; but it is even more possible to argue that it had been the trials and savage sentencing in Scotland which had lit the fuse among reformers in the south. Unlike the extra-parliamentary agitation going on in Ireland at the same time, that of Scotland was closely connected to London. Many of the leading members of the LCS were Scots, beginning with Hardy himself, and of course English reformers had been among those who suffered heavy penalties in the wake of the breaking-up of the British convention in Edinburgh.

Dundas himself had been in Scotland from late October to late November 1792 and had sent back to Pitt via Nepean a steady stream of reports of simmering unrest, outbreaks of violence, and popular protest, and of the proliferation of political societies.[21] He had made his view plain then. He was more than satisfied 'that unless something effectual can be done to check the indiscriminate practice of associations, they will spread the fermentation of the country to such a height it will be impossible to restrain the effects of them'.[22]

By 'something effectual', Dundas obviously meant active coercion. When he travelled down from Scotland to attend to urgent affairs in London in late November, he left behind him William Pulteney, M.P. for Bath, to advise his nephew Robert Dundas, the lord advocate of Scotland, and to spearhead an operation to galvanize the support of the property-owning gentry for the government. By 2 January 1793 Muir was under arrest. 'The great object', Robert Dundas wrote to his uncle, 'is to satisfy the country that within the British dominions none of these fellows are safe, and that every exertion will be made by government to bring them to justice'.[23]

But it was the pursuit of the supporters of the idea of convention, given a new meaning by the Jacobin-style meetings in Edinburgh, which focused the activities of the authorities and which led to most of the London arrests. Both the LCS and the SCI had sent delegates to the British convention in Edinburgh in October 1793: Charles Sinclair, Henry Redhead Yorke, Joseph Gerrald, and Maurice Margarot, the last two of whom had suffered at the hands of the Scottish courts. Indeed it would seem that the major criterion for inclusion on the list of the thirteen was that they had been identified as having constituted a joint LCS/SCI Committee of Secrecy or Committee of Correspondence formed on 11 April 1794 with the aim of establishing a national convention in London, as indeed the LCS mass meeting at Chalk Farm on 14 April resolved. It is this which explains the apparent arbitrariness of indicting such a patently harmless individual as Thomas Holcroft while failing to indict more obvious candidates like the notorious John Frost. The fact that, on the only occasion when Holcroft appeared at a committee meeting, he prevented any business at all from taking place by giving a lengthy disquisition about improving the human mind does not seem to have deflected the prosecution from its purpose.[24]

The committee included Thelwall, Moore, Hodgson, Baxter, Joyce (secretary), Wardle, Kyd, Holcroft, Lovett, and Horne Tooke's close friend William Sharp. There was also a subsidiary list: Ashley, Bonney, J. Pearson, and Horne Tooke, who were all taken into custody.[25] Of the thirteen proceeded against for high treason, the only two not directly identified with the committee were Hardy and Richter. Hardy, as secretary of the LCS, had of course signed the letter of 27 March which officially approached the SCI with the plan of a convention and the request to 'act in conjunction' to that end.[26] Richter had read the resolutions at the LCS meeting at Chalk Farm on 14 April which had called for a national convention. Sharp furthermore informed the Privy Council on 24 May that Richter was one of the 'violent men' of the movement, like Gerrald and Margarot. Presumably it was due to his volunteering information such as this that Sharp escaped prosecution. He had been selected to join the committee, he said, only because he was a friend of Horne Tooke's, and it had been Horne Tooke's arguments which had helped to convince SCI members of the honourable credentials of the LCS delegates.[27]

Horne Tooke himself had been named by the spy John Taylor as having been selected to join the committee;[28] but, spending most of his time at Wimbledon, he had evidently declined, nominating Sharp in his stead, presumably to act as his proxy and keep the lid on things. Horne Tooke had certainly never approved of the British convention in Edinburgh, nor of sending SCI delegates; neither had his friend Sharp — nor Kyd, nor Joyce for that matter. This was later demonstrated at the trial, at least to the satisfaction of the jury. Indeed there is every possibility that Horne Tooke's intention was to scupper the committee from within or at least to manipulate it in the direction he wished it to go. As it was, the LCS delegates were not happy with the SCI and denounced it for its tardiness.[29] Certainly something of a power struggle was going on between the two societies and Horne Tooke was probably at the centre of it. The authorities, with minds perhaps not as subtle as Horne Tooke's, saw only that he was the linch-pin of the association between the two societies and, in the context of the Chalk Farm meeting of 14 April, and then of the SCI dinner of 2 May at the Crown and Anchor tavern, were able to convince themselves of their case.

'Convention' was definitely the key word; but the charge of high treason was hysterical and the product not of considered legal opinion but of the reports of the House of Commons's Committee of Secrecy of 16 May and 6 June, which used the language of sensation and spoke of traitorous, daring, and desperate designs of the most serious magnitude, claiming to have concrete evidence from the impounded documents of the two societies of a planned insurrection in order to obtain a change in the legislature. Such a change, so achieved, could hardly, argued the committee, 'be supposed to stop short of an entire destruction of the Constitution'.

A Proposition so extravagant may at first be difficult to be credited; but it appears to the Committee to be distinctly proved, from an Examination of the Nature of the Principles themselves; from a consideration of the System as actually carried into Effect in France, and proposed as a Model by those who were the chief Actors in these Proceedings in this Country; and, by repeated Declarations or Acts, which either directly or by necessary Inference point at the Destruction of Hereditary Monarchy, Hereditary Nobility, and every Distinction of Orders and Ranks in Society.[30]

Reports drawn up by a committee of the House of Lords echoed the same sentiments. On the strength of the first House of Commons report, Habeas Corpus was suspended and the way made clear for wholesale judicial repression.

At this stage, however, no specific charges against the accused were made, since no intrinsically traitorous act could be established. Those committed to the Tower or to Newgate were held only on suspicion of treasonable practices. It was now up to the prosecution's legal team to convert suspicion of treason into indictable treason: a process which involved radical departures from legal precedent and which fuelled the speculation that the government was preparing proceedings against hundreds more people (Hardy believed in a figure of 800) pending the precedent which would hopefully be established by the convictions of the thirteen.

The prosecution eventually mounted its case on the basis of what was termed, by the defence, 'constructive' treason. The forming of a national convention, it was argued, would by its very nature imperil the life of the king even though no plot actually to harm or overthrow the king could be proved. This approach was espoused, apparently with some vehemence, in the Privy Council by the lord chief justice of the common pleas, Sir James Eyre, who was later to preside at the trials.[31] But the ultimate responsibility for the charge of high treason belonged to the attorney general, Sir John Scott. As Lord Eldon, he argued years later that, had the charge been merely sedition, firstly the public would not have had the opportunity to have had laid before them the full extent of the danger to the state and constitution; and secondly, had treason been proved in a trial for sedition, this could have led to an acquittal (for sedition) and prejudiced the crown's case in an ensuing treason trial.[32] Neither explanation has ever been considered convincing.[33] Reading between the lines suggests, however, that he was under some pressure, and, in view of the language of government in parliament (Pitt headed the Committee of Secrecy and presented the report), the decision to prosecute for high treason probably came directly from Pitt and his new ex-Whig lord chancellor, Loughborough.[34] The preamble to the Habeas Corpus Suspension Act which became law on 23 May itself referred to a 'traitorous and detestable conspiracy . . . formed for subverting the existing Laws and Constitution, and for introducing the system of anarchy and confusion which has so fatally prevailed in France'. It was only on 18 July 1794 that the Privy Council directed that the judges be assembled by the lord chief justice of the King's Bench, Lord Kenyon, in order to 'consider and report their opinion what may be the most speedy way of proceeding for the Tryal of the persons in custody'.[35] The product of their deliberations was no doubt acceptable to the government, but arguably ensured acquittal as well as curtailing the range of the government's future options in the continuing campaign against dissident domestic opinion.

As the trials of the thirteen men approached, their symbolic importance as test cases became more and more apparent in a climate of mounting tension. In June parliament passed the London Militia Bill, which made ratepayers subject to conscription by ballot. This was highly unpopular not least since it was felt that the burden fell unequally, only those who were balloted for militia service being required to find and pay for their substitutes. This measure was inextricably bound up in the public mind with the practice of crimping, whereby agents received bounty money for military recruits, who were frequently procured by criminal and often violent methods. With the great increase in the size of the British military establishment the bounties went up accordingly, providing even greater incentive for the outrages of the crimps. Public hostility finally overflowed into the worst series of disturbances seen in London since the Gordon riots of 1780. Patrick Colquhoun, who as magistrate at the Worship Street police office played a significant part in policing the riots, let his opinion be known to government that, on the basis of some handbills he had discovered, the political societies were deeply implicated.[36]

Then in August and September came the treason trials in Scotland of Robert Watt and James Downie — finally ringing down the curtain on the Scottish conventions episode with the convictions of both men. The lord advocate Robert Dundas, showing some sensitivity to professional legal opinion, made certain that Braxfield did not preside at this trial. Perhaps too, Dundas was particularly keen not to aggravate public opinion and open up any debate on behalf of Watt, a man who had once been on his uncle's payroll as a spy.[37] Watt was duly hanged with little public sympathy just a few days before the London trials were about to begin, and Downie, although convicted, was later conditionally pardoned.

But there was to be more sensation in advance of the commencement of the trials of the thirteen. On 28 September, only five days before the court was due to be convened, Paul Thomas Lemaitre, George Higgins, and John Smith, all members of the LCS, were arrested on suspicion of a plot to assassinate the king. On the testimony of an informer, Thomas Upton, also a member of the LCS, the plan was to have involved using a brass tube, or pop-gun, to fire from close range, either at the theatre or at Windsor, a poison dart at the king. Interrogations before the Privy Council dwelt as heavily on the Committee of Secrecy of the LCS/SCI as they did upon the convoluted technicalities of the plot to kill the king,[38] suggesting that the government had not given up on trying to establish a genuine threat to the king as opposed to a constructive one. Certainly it was felt by many that the Pop-gun Plot had been entirely fabricated to support the government's case against the thirteen by implication.[39] Certainly, notwithstanding the bizarre, even unbelievable, nature of the plot, the prosecution did apparently consider using it in its case.[40]

As it was, the three trials which actually took place, those of Hardy, Horne Tooke, and Thelwall, were conducted, especially that of Horne Tooke, with great propriety and even good humour, allowing those who wished it to see the acquittals as the best proof possible of the superiority of the British system over that of revolutionary France. Others argued, however, that it was only the courts which protected the traditional rights of Englishmen from a government poised to use terror to crush dissent and re-institute pre-1688-style arbitrary executive rule. Clive Emsley suggests, cautiously, that such claims against Pitt and his cabinet may have been more hysterical than real, citing the relatively low figures for actual prosecutions.[41] Yet it is difficult not to sense government over-reaction, even panic, which, translated into the potentially brutal zeal of men like Dundas and Reeves, might well have required sobering reminders of legal limitations. Indeed, had the courts convicted, subsequent events might have been very different.

There was in élite circles considerable disgust with what was considered to be Eyre's conciliatory demeanour at the trials — in sharp contrast to his previously unequivocal attitude in the Privy Council when, as we have already seen, he had been instrumental in shaping the form and substance of the prosecution case of constructive treason. Lord Granville Leveson, a future office-holder who was present at Horne Tooke's trial, although he did not believe Eyre affected the outcome, commented nevertheless that the lord chief justice had 'manifested a great partiality to the Prisoner' and that 'people in general complain loudly of the evident wishes that he evinced of being popular with him and his democratic adherents'.[42] Lord Glenbervie, who had been present at most of the Privy Council interrogations, remarked that it had been Horne Tooke who seemed the accuser and Eyre the accused. He recalled a story told him by government placeman, George Rose, which suggests that Pitt too was less than pleased with the judge. After the trials Eyre had been pointedly snubbed by Pitt, which had so agitated him that, on a carriage journey with Rose to his country house, he 'talked of it [the snub] . . . with such a degree of vexation and despondency as absolutely to sob and cry during a great part of way . . . He [Rose] vows to God and unfeignedly believes without a particle of doubt that this chagrin and mortification killed him [Eyre]. He certainly died soon after and made way for Lord Alvanley . . . '.[43] Eyre died in 1799.

The question might be asked, 'why Eyre?'. Why not the lord chief justice of the King's Bench, Lord Kenyon, a much more hardline hanging judge than Eyre? Two possible reasons suggest themselves. In the first place, Kenyon may have been unhappy with Eyre's constructive treason ploy and preferred the lesser charge of sedition which would, at least almost certainly, have resulted in convictions. In this he may have been overruled. In the second, it is possible that Pitt, Loughborough, or Scott (or all three) may not have thought Kenyon capable of handling so clever a man as Horne Tooke, having demonstrated in the 1792 action for debt, Charles James Fox v. John Horne Tooke (arising out of Tooke's petition regarding the outcome of the elections for Westminster of 1790), an inability to cope with the would-be barrister in the courtroom and allowing him on that occasion virtually to direct the proceedings and use the opportunity for a prolonged and virulent attack upon government corruption.[44] Certainly a repeat of that performance would not have been relished by the crown. Indeed John Lord Campbell later recalled that the original plan had been to try the prisoners before Kenyon in the Court of the King's Bench, 'but some apprehension was entertained of his intemperance of manner, and they were arraigned at the Old Bailey before that quiet and safe Judge, Chief Justice Eyre'.[45]

Horne Tooke's trial began on Monday 17 November and ended on

22 November 1794. It took a jury, largely consisting of Patriotic Association men if we are to believe *The New Annual Register*, less than eight minutes to acquit him. This was not wholly the result of masterful defence tactics. The momentum toward acquittal was well established even before the trial had actually commenced.

It had begun with the opening of the special commission of oyer and terminer at the session house, Clerkenwell, on 2 October, at which Lord Justice Eyre delivered his charge to the grand jury and dismissed it 'with confident expectation that your judgment will be directed to those conclusions which may clear innocent men from all suspicion of guilt, bring the guilty to condign punishment, preserve the life of our gracious sovereign, secure stability of our government, and maintain the public peace, in which comprehensive term is included the welfare and happiness of the people under the protection of the laws and liberties of the kingdom'. In other words, 'confident' that they would find true bills against all of those charged. The prisoners, who were not present at this stage in the proceedings, did not hear Eyre put to the grand jury the case that reform societies could 'degenerate, and become unlawful in the highest degree, even to the enormous extent of High Treason' and explain patiently the logic behind the charge that the accused had, indeed, according to the statute, 25 Edw. III, compassed and imagined the death of the king:

I presume that I have sufficiently explained to you that a *project to bring people together in convention in imitation of those National Conventions in France in order to usurp the government of the country*, and *any one step taken towards bringing it about*, such as for instance, 'consultation, forming of committees to consider of means, acting in those committees', would be a case of no difficulty that it would be the *clearest High Treason*; it would be compassing and imagining the King's death and destruction of all order, religion, laws, all property, all security for the lives and liberties of the king's subjects.[46]

Then followed in the more usual language of the court the listing of the overt acts required as proof of such compassing and imagining: nine of them, and all related to the activities of the SCI and LCS. The first four concerned the preparations for the convention (meeting, writing, publishing), five, six, seven, and nine concerned the collection of arms and conspiring at insurrection, and the eighth charge concerned distributing literature in order to incite and direct insurrection among the subjects of 'our said Lord the King'.

An important tactical victory for the defence emerged from this opening day of the special commission: the publication, anonymously, in the Foxite *Morning Chronicle* on 21 October of William Godwin's 'Cursory Strictures on the Charge delivered by Lord Chief Justice Eyre to the Grand Jury', a powerful attack on Eyre's legal conceit of constructive treason, a treason, he declared, completely without legal precedent, and 'first discovered by Chief Justice Eyre in 1794'. He accused Eyre of ' . . . wild conjecture, . . . premature presumption, imaginations . . . licentious, and dreams . . . full of sanguinary and tremendous prophecy'.

Godwin anticipated the defence argument that, as far as the convention was concerned, 'twelve or fourteen years ago, many of his Majesty's present ministers were deeply engaged in a project of this nature' and went on to castigate the judiciary not only for prejudging the case but for usurping the role of parliament in finding fresh treasons beyond the scope of 25 Edw. III.

He attacked the practice of causing men to be subjected to anxiety, ignominy, obloquy, and the ultimate risk of standing trial with the possibility of partial judges and ignorant juries (an obvious reference to the Scottish trials), simply in an attempt to set a precedent that would stand in future cases. He wound up his attack both upon the intellectual basis of the prosecution's charge of treason and the proceedings of the special commission itself with the speech he suggested Eyre should make to the accused:

Six months ago you engaged in measures, which you believ'd conducive to the public good. You examin'd them in the sincerity of your hearts, and you admitted them with the full conviction of the understanding. You adopted them from this ruling motive, the love of your country and mankind. You had no warning that the measures in which you engaged were acts of High Treason; no law told you so; no precedent recorded it; no man existing upon the face of the earth could have predicted such an interpretation. You went to your beds with a perfect and full conviction, that you had acted upon the principles of immutable justice, and that you had offended no provision or statute that was ever devised. I the judge sitting upon the bench, you, Gentlemen of the Jury, every inhabitant of the island of Great Britain, had just as much reason to conceive they were incurring the penalties of the law, as the prisoners at the bar. This is the nature of the crime: These are the circumstances of the case.

And for this, the sentence of the Court (but not of the law) is, *that you, and each of you*, shall be taken from the bar, and conveyed to the place from whence you came, and from thence be drawn upon a hurdle to the place of execution, there to be hanged by the neck, but not until you are dead; you shall be taken down alive, your privy members shall be cut off and your bowels shall be taken out and burnt before your faces; your hearts shall be severed from your bodies, and your bodies shall then be divided into four quarters, which are to be at the King's disposal; and the Lord have mercy on your souls![47]

That the full extent of the rituals of punishment for treason were no longer carried out, that hanging and beheading were thought to suffice in that age of reason hardly detracted from Godwin's message — that Eyre's charge was a legal trap meant to dispose arbitrarily of innocent men. Quite apart from the quality of the argument, the fact that it took up virtually the entire issue of the *Morning Chronicle* was impressive, and indicative of the intense interest generated by the prosecutions.

On 6 October the grand jury returned a true bill against all except John Lovett. On 7 October, however, the solemnity of the proceedings was somewhat rudely shattered by the appearance of Thomas Holcroft, who demanded that, since he was named as one of the indicted, he be taken into custody and tried accordingly. This threw the court into disarray and created a degree of levity as the bench argued the toss as to whether Holcroft was genuinely the

Holcroft of the indictment and whether it was in his best interest to place himself in custody.[48] After some unseemly indecision he was eventually taken into custody and committed to Newgate, but he had won a good psychological and tactical advantage for the defence, as Alexander Stephens acknowledged much later in his *Memoirs of John Horne Tooke*.

Those in custody, Hardy, Horne Tooke, Thelwall, Richter, Bonney, Kyd, Joyce, Baxter, and now Holcroft (Moore, Wardle, and Hodgson having evaded custody) met together for the first time at their arraignment at the Old Bailey on 25 October. Horne Tooke told Holcroft 'that the best thing our prosecution could have done, for the cause of freedom, was that which they had done; imprison and indict us; except the still better thing which they had yet to do; namely hang us'.[49] And John Baxter, a 'little fellow' whom Horne Tooke later declared he had never seen before, 'a hero', stepped up to him and said, 'Mr. Tooke, our lives have hitherto been but of little service to our country; let us then behave like men, and see, if by dying bravely, we cannot prove of some service to the commonwealth'.[50] Horne Tooke also took the opportunity to complain of the lack of warning of their removal from the Tower to Newgate, with the resultant loss of an opportunity for consultation with his counsel, with whom he was meant to have dined in the Tower the previous day, and of the disorder and confusion into which all his papers had been thrown by the removal.[51] Horne Tooke evidently did not mean to accept martyrdom without a fight.

Hardy's was the first of the trials to take place, commencing on 27 October at the Old Bailey and, as Gibbs insisted at Horne Tooke's trial, it was obviously intended to be the prosecution's show piece, not least because a conviction would have been used in the ensuing trials as major evidence of the existence of a conspiracy. As it turned out Hardy was acquitted, and of course this fact was used to some effect by Gibbs on behalf of Horne Tooke. If Hardy, whom the crown obviously perceived to have been the 'arch-conspirator, . . . the leader of all the others, and the person who set all this imputed mischief on foot', if Hardy, who was meant to have so conspired with Horne Tooke to overturn the government, was proved innocent, then there was no conspiracy at all and Horne Tooke was likewise innocent. The verdict that acquitted Hardy absolved his alleged co-conspirator also.[52]

There can be little doubt that Hardy's acquittal completely altered the conduct of Horne Tooke's trial. The kind of self-conscious heroics that the arraignment had promised did not materialize, nor did the righteous vituperation, nor (except occasionally) the intellectual bullying so characteristic of Horne Tooke's previous encounters with the courts. It was with a professional, even cool, detachment that he, with his counsel, Erskine and Gibbs, set about demolishing the crown's case — a posture that would have been a very unlikely one had Hardy been convicted. Sir Beaumont Hotham, a baron of the exchequer, wrote to Lord Auckland on 15 November, ten days after the acquittal of Hardy:

At eight o'clock on Monday morning we proceed, under the special commission, to the trial of Horne Tooke, who asked the Sheriffs yesterday, when they went to visit him, that he might be invited to dine up stairs with the Lord Mayor and Judges on the day of his acquittal. Free and easy! He has no doubt of his acquittal, nor have I, after Hardy's. I wish you would come to town, and try if the country can be saved.[53]

As it was, the trial turned into something of a chic circus, with a string of prominent men called before it to perform what must have been, for some of them, demeaning tricks on behalf of the defence. The list included the duke of Richmond, Major Cartwright, Charles James Fox, Philip Francis, Sheridan, Earl Stanhope, the Revd. Christopher Wyvill, Earl Camden, Lord Frederick Campbell, and Richard Beadon, the bishop of Gloucester. But it must have been the spectacle of the prime minister himself having difficulty with his recollections which gave the most entertainment value to the packed courthouse audience. Horne Tooke himself cross-examined the prime minister, extracting, in spite of his being prevented by Eyre from reading to the court a letter of Pitt's on the subject of reform, the vital admission that Pitt had himself been party to a 'convention of delegates appointed by different counties and great towns in England' in May 1782 at the reform meeting at Thatched House tavern when Pitt and Horne Tooke had both been present.[54] It was generally acknowledged that Horne Tooke had probably delivered the best performance of his career to date: a model of cool, intelligent, good-humoured circumspection with little evidence of the sneering iconoclast — of the 'philosophical viper' — that many in the establishment had been expecting.[55]

The trials virtually brought to an end Thomas Hardy's brief career as a working-class leader but for John Horne Tooke it was simply the most dramatic incident — by no means the climax — of forty years of political activism. Pitt's instincts in striking at Tooke, as P. A. Brown remarked, were correct. He was 'the heart of the reform movement'.[56] Tooke's influence on the younger generation of radical reformers — men like John Thelwall, Thomas Hardy, Felix Vaughan, John Richter, and, later, Sir Francis Burdett — was of major importance, and he remained, till his death, in the eyes of many one of the most celebrated legends of the reform movement.

He was born John Horne on 25 June 1736 (he adopted the name Tooke in 1792 at the request of a patron, William Tooke of Purley), the third son of John Horne, a wealthy London poulterer. Destined for the church by his upwardly mobile parents, he was educated, first at the Soho Square Academy, next at Westminster School, and then at Eton, where he apparently learned some basic lessons in political warfare. In 1754 he went up to St. John's College, Cambridge, and in 1756 entered the Inner Temple in London with the idea of pursuing a career in law.

Forced by family pressures, however, he withdrew, and was ordained as a priest of the Church of England in 1760. Notwithstanding a love of cards, colourful clothes, and company, he was for several years the moderately assiduous incumbent of the living his father had bought him at New Brentford, Middlesex. Politics, however, in the form of the great Wilkite ructions of 1765, soon claimed him on behalf of the Wilkite cause.

My Heart, in its first Pantings, beat to LIBERTY. *She* is twisted with my Heartstrings, and cannot be torn from thence.

They have formed together a GORDIAN Knot, which cannot be *untwisted* by the subtle Finger of CORRUPTION, nor *loosened* by the Touch of FEAR. Nothing can separate us. No! not the cruel and bloody SWORD of TYRANNY.

Her Union with me is lovely and honourable thro' Life; and even in Death I will not be divided from her.[57]

John Horne Tooke was a man typical in many ways of his historical moment. He was born into the middle classes at a time when the decomposition and flux of the English class system of the past three hundred years was attaining crisis point without, as yet, any real understanding having been reached of the class nature of social and political inequality. He was born at a time when social and political pressures were bringing into focus the question of the relationship between the individual and the state, without there yet being any clear perception of the political issues involved in such a relationship. Like Peter Wentworth, Sir Edward Coke, and Sir John Eliot, the opponents of Elizabeth I and James I, he set himself to combat the encroachments of the future with a mind overstocked with the pedantries of the past. What had happened in the years since Coke's time, the civil war, the restoration, the revolution of 1688, the Act of Settlement, had provided not new insights but a refurbished stock of political myth. The law and the constitution were to be held on to, as the only true barriers to the enormities of communal change. Neither the political implications of existing law nor the possibilities inherent in change were questioned or explored. Horne Tooke's political code was essentially unimaginative and rigid but rendered sporadically alluring by his flair for making debating points and for manipulating forensic detail. In this respect Horne Tooke was typical of many reforming radicals of his day, from Wilkes to Henry Hunt — ready enough to question the fundamentals of the power structure erecting itself over their heads, but resolutely ignoring all possibility of examining the platform of social and economic privilege on which they themselves stood. Arguably Horne Tooke's stand upon outraged principles, like those of Wilkes and Henry Hunt, derived more from natural pugnacity, perhaps even outraged vanity and conceit, than from any coherent political theory. Certainly their platform was almost completely negative and dissentient, and the alternative policies they proposed aimed more at restoration of mythical liberties lost than at any future utopia to be gained. Indeed it is tempting to see them as selfish egotists who wished only to be left alone, unmolested by Behemoth, in possession of their fantasies about sturdy Anglo-Saxon yeomen — before the imposition of the Norman yoke — in glorious possession of their just and eternal rights. But this would not be quite fair. It was not until Bentham and utilitarianism that a more powerful intellectual model was constructed with which to carry forward middle-class political ambition; and in any case originality has seldom ever been the strongest quality of individuals in the vanguard of direct political action. Nor has humility.

Tooke's politics have been described as 'those of the old-fashioned city patriots'[58] and all which that entails: anti-Whig-aristocracy; emphatically if not fanatically Protestant; middle-class; nationalist; pro-commerce and anti-court; but essentially conservative — undemocratic in the broadest sense — shrinking from the idea of violent revolution. Certainly, the masses never formed a part of Horne Tooke's scheme of parliamentary reform. Their involvement in the political arena was for him 'improper and impractical'.[59] He would always, he told a court in 1777, 'rather hear the mob hiss than halloo',[60] and another court heard in 1794 how he had often said he would much rather be governed by St. James's than by St. Giles's.[61] In the matter of universal suffrage, then, he differed intrinsically from his friend and political associate John Cartwright, and from Hardy and the LCS. But he loathed the non-democrat Fox, against whom he stood for Westminster (unsuccessfully) in 1790 and 1796. More than anything else Tooke's politics were personal and confrontational. They were a form of combat in which he pitted himself against authority not only on behalf of his ideals but on behalf of his intellect.

His conviction in 1777 for libel and subsequent imprisonment following his advertisements to raise money for the widows and orphans of American rebels murdered by British troops at Lexington disturbed him not so much because it was unjust as because he had lost a contest of wits, in which he had been betrayed, not by the forces of arbitrary tyranny, but by '*two prepositions and a conjunction*'.[62] From this followed his famous letter from prison to his old Cambridge friend John Dunning (later Lord Ashburton) concerning the uses and abuses of language, out of which grew his great philological treatise, *The Diversions of Purley*, a work which established him securely in the intellectual firmament of his day as the Newton (or Locke) of language, and even among society dilettanti as something of a literary lion. Henrietta, countess of Bessborough, wrote to Lord Granville Leveson in 1805 that she was reading a 'strange book — Horne Tooke's 2^d Vol. of the Diversions of Purley'. (The first part had been published in 1786, and issued in a second edition in 1798. The countess was evidently reading part II, which was published in 1805.) She thought it 'impudent, ingenious, indecent and entertaining — that is, its extreme ingenuity and sometimes its impudence amuses, when its coarseness and indelicacy does not disgust, or too long a list of words tire'.[63] But the fundamental theoretical premise that inspired the work — put crudely, that all language can be reduced to material objects — has not obtained the approval of modern students of linguistics.[64] Language was ultimately too complex a system to be contained within Tooke's essentially narrow intellectual perspective. It is, nevertheless, worth considering whether, if Horne Tooke had freed himself from his self-imposed burden regarding language, he might have directed his political energies more fruitfully, developing perhaps the philosophical framework that was so obviously missing from reform activity of this period. Thomas Spence's excursions into spelling reform certainly did not prevent him from formulating a fundamental political ideology, but then Spence was first and foremost a visionary and in any case Spence's interest in language was as a corollary of his political ideals, not as the embodiment of them.

But in Horne Tooke as a political figure this other dimension of intellect and his self-conscious awareness of its superiority were what made him unique. Kept well honed among his intellectual friends at Wimbledon, his gifts of incisive observation and sardonic wit were powerful weapons when deployed elsewhere, making him much sought after by the less endowed of his own political persuasion and by those, like Thomas Hardy, of somewhat more extreme opinions. Incapable of the imaginative or intuitive leap that produced Tom Paine's *The Rights of Man*, nevertheless he developed habits of intellectual enquiry and forensic analysis which gave to his criticisms of the upper-class political hegemony a clarity and pungency that was compelling, whatever they may have lacked in depth of understanding.

It might be argued, however, that intellectual gamesmanship played almost as large a part in his career as political conviction did. That possibility tempts us to wonder at times whether he took his own political platform as seriously as his contemporaries obviously believed he did. But, if he was a joker at heart, he found nothing remotely amusing in his arrest and imprisonment for high treason in 1794 — a fact which his prison diary establishes in contrast to the vision of irrepressible insouciance which the press continued to delight in. And it was the underlying consistency, to the point of rigidity, of his basic political ideas over forty years which he was able in court to prove and which materially aided in his acquittal. Finally in 1801, having been returned to parliament by Lord Camelford as representative of a rotten borough, Old Sarum, he was thrown out by an act, brought in on his account, to bar clergymen from sitting in the House of Commons. This last event was not merely the result of spite or even of distaste for the company of an 'unconvicted felon', as William Windham persisted in calling him. The establishment still genuinely feared him, although he had proved by then to be something of a paper tiger.[65]

Horne Tooke never married, although he had at least three illegitimate children, the two Misses Hart, Mary and Charlotte, who lived with him till his death, and a son, a Mr. Montague, who went into the service of the East India Company but with whom Horne Tooke appeared to lose contact. His unmarried state does not seem to have been the result of any misogyny on his part — his biographer Alexander Stephens makes a point of stressing his courtly charm — but it may have been the consequence of sensitivity regarding his life-long bowel problem, which necessitated, it would seem, regular external aid for defecation. Whether his problem was physical or psychological we shall never know. But perhaps he felt it was too much, in any case, for the weaker sex to endure.

He died in 1812. He had had, he said, a happy life. Certainly he died in comfort in his own home at Wimbledon at a fairly advanced age, surrounded by family and friends, a testimony of a kind to his personal qualities, but even more a testimony to the goodwill of a British jury in the year 1794.

Tooke's career suggests that he was no mere ideologue or fellow-traveller. Whatever else he might have said or done, he believed in what he believed with an inflexibility tested by the fire of real sacrifice, and with a long-term consistency not evident in the careers of his early companions in struggle, of his old friend John Wilkes (from whom he soon parted), or of his disciple, Sir Francis Burdett (in whose arms he died). Tooke's brand of conviction politics was dressed up often enough in historical mythology and legalistic pedantry, but perhaps what it ultimately boiled down to was simply a belief in independence, individualism, and opposition for their own sakes. In some ways he was simply the embodiment of British bloody-mindedness. His self-consciousness and sometimes his self-pity irritate, his insights into the rottenness of a political order which has since passed away perplex us with their apparent irrelevance to our own times, his lack of constructive vision disappoints. Yet, arguably, Horne Tooke's place in English political history is obscure and perplexing to us today, simply because, although he himself was not aware of it, his cause had already been won. The bourgeois political culture for which he had failed to find an intellectual rationale was already effectively in place. In spite of the seeming victory of aristocratic privilege and of the party of Pitt and the royal prerogative in the years of the French wars and immediately afterwards, that bourgeois political culture moved, without any revolution, relatively peacefully, into a position of hegemony in 1832. In comparison with more romantic figures of dissent —Theobald Wolfe Tone say, or Thomas Paine — whose appeal to us today rests perhaps more upon their ultimate failure than upon their success and whose arguments (respectively, Irish republicanism and English republicanism) are still intelligible to us, precisely because they are still the subject of debate, Horne Tooke's life-long struggle may seem peculiarly irrelevant. Yet in an era when the British system of parliamentary democracy is once again attracting persistent criticism for its failure to achieve fair representation of the people and when the state is routinely accused of taking to itself powers which both reduce its accountability and stifle legitimate dissent, is it not time, perhaps, to take a longer, harder look at John Horne Tooke?

At some stage previous to his arrest Horne Tooke had had a copy of the first edition of part I of *The Diversions of Purley* bound up with interleaved blank pages in order to facilitate his preparation of a second edition. He had this volume with him in the Tower of London and used many of the interleaved pages to record the details of his imprisonment between 16 May and 22 November 1794. This volume is now in the British Library (shelf mark C. 60. i. 15). In

1897, prior to its acquisition by the British Library, G.J.W. (possibly George Wallas), having gained temporary access to it, published substantial extracts from the diary in several instalments in *Notes and Queries* (Eighth Series 11 (January–June 1897), beginning in no. 263 (9 January 1897), 21–22), but took little trouble with it except to expurgate Horne Tooke's vulgarities. None of the letters were transcribed and there were many other omissions and some significant errors. This is thus the first time the diary has been published *in extenso* and provided with detailed notes.

The format of the diary is complicated by Tooke's editorial notes, mostly of a later date, for the second edition of part I of *The Diversions of Purley* (these have been omitted from the present publication) and by jottings which Tooke made at the time of his imprisonment but which are not part of the narrative of the diary as such. These latter sometimes take the form of elaborate financial calculations, reminders to himself of various bills to be paid or of money owed him, and lists of names. Mostly they have been omitted. There are also frequent incursions on to the printed pages of *The Diversions of Purley* itself. Where these are obviously within the context of the diary narrative, they have been included, but have been printed in a smaller point size. Where they are Tooke's editorial notes on *The Diversions of Purley*, they have been omitted altogether.

By and large, the main note sequence at the end of the text attempts to identify persons mentioned by Tooke and to give background information on points raised by his narrative. Biographical details of significant individuals who are mentioned in the diary appear in the Biographical Index.

NOTES TO INTRODUCTION

The following abbreviations have been used for classes of records in the Public Record Office (PRO): TS for Treasury Solicitor's papers; HO for Home Office papers; PC for Privy Council papers.

[1]   *The Parliamentary Register; or History of the Proceedings and Debates of the House of Commons; . . . during the Fourth Session of the Seventeenth Parliament of Great Britain*, vol. XXXVIII (London, 1794), pp. 245–53 (Friday 16th May).

[2]   British Library, Additional MS 37874 fo. 33.

[3]   P. A. Brown, *The French Revolution in English History* (London, 1918), pp. 22–23.

[4]   In this period the SCI's first meeting at the Crown and Anchor was on 18 May 1792. Those recorded as present were: Major Cartwright (chairman); Mr. Tooke; Mr. Aspinall; Mr. Merry; Mr. Pearson; Lord Daer; Mr. Martin; Mr. Paine; Mr. Joseph Gerrald; Mr. Lloyd; Mr. Sturch; Dr. Edwards; Mr. Sharpe (Charlotte Street); Mr. Bush; Mr. J. Adams; Mr. Lockhart; Captain T[ooke] Harwood; Mr. Batley; Mr. J. A. Batley; Mr. Favell; Mr. Williams; Mr. Frost; Mr. Hull; Mr. Cooper; Mr. Watts; Mr. Campbell; Mr. Fitzgerald; Mr. Tuffin; Mr. William Sharp. At this meeting Mr. John Belmanno, Mr. Thos. Lloyd, Mr. George Williams, Captain Broome, Gerrald Rutt, and Mr. George Ansell were elected members, and Messrs. Charles Sinclair and Joseph Johnson were proposed. (PRO TS 11/962)

[5]   See Kathleen Wilson, 'Inventing revolution: 1688 and eighteenth-century popular politics', *Journal of British Studies*, 28 : 4(1989), 349–86. For the role of Enlightenment values on the reform movement, see also Marianne Elliott, *Wolfe Tone: prophet of Irish independence* (New Haven and London, 1989), pp. 20–21.

[6]   The Privy Council interviewed Captain George Munro very early on to obtain information about English reformers' activities in Paris. He volunteered that he had seen Frost, Barlow, Stone, Joyce, and a Mr. Skill at the national convention of France 'on the occasion of presenting . . . an address from the society for Constitutional Information'. (PRO PC 2/140 14 May)

[7a] Alexander Stephens, *Memoirs of J. Horne Tooke*, 2 vols. (London, 1813), II, pp. 112–13n.

[7b] 'The Trial of Thomas Hardy for High Treason', in T. B. and T. J. Howell (compilers), *A Complete Collection of State Trials and Proceedings for High Treason and Other Crimes and Misdemeanors*, 33 vols. (London, 1816–26), XXIV (34 & 35 George III . . . A.D. 1794) (London, 1818), cols. 529–30.

[8]   Thomas Holcroft, *A Narrative of Facts, relating to a Prosecution for High Treason* (London, 1795), p. 9.

[9]   Holcroft, op. cit. (note 8), p. 11.

[10] Holcroft, op. cit. (note 8), p. 14.

[11] Reeves's association was not a society in the same sense as the SCI and LCS, both of which had a constitution and an open membership. Initially it probably consisted of Reeves — and persons selected by him for specific tasks. Employees of the Post Office provided vital services in disseminating printed propaganda on pain of dismissal for failure to do so. And the directing committee, when it *was* formed, consisted of individuals who were not so much volunteers as handpicked conscripts: prominent men in law and commerce who rarely dared to decline the invitation and whose job was to organize and legitimize the intimidation of political dissidents. An early member, the eminent lawyer Thomas Law, who complained of the committee's methods, especially the use of anonymous information, upon resigning, publicly denounced Reeves before smartly removing himself to America (Thomas Law, *A Letter to Mr. Reeves, Chairman of the Association for Preserving Liberty and*

Property (London, 1793)). In the provinces similar groups of local worthies formed associations and busied themselves in collecting and disseminating information and harassing local Jacobins like the prominent cotton merchant Thomas Walker of Manchester, who, although acquitted of conspiracy in 1794, was financially ruined.

[12] George Croly, 'The Life of a Democrat: a sketch of John Horne Tooke. Part II', *Blackwood's Edinburgh Magazine*, 34, no. 211 (August 1834), 220.

[13] See Henry W. Meikle, *Scotland and the French Revolution* (Glasgow, 1912), for an account of the Scottish and British conventions.

[14] William Adam brought three motions before the House of Commons (14 February, 10 March, and 25 March), seeking government intervention in the cases of Muir and Fyshe Palmer; but to no avail.

[15a] *The Proceedings at Large on the Trial of John Horne Tooke for High Treason taken in short-hand by J. H. Blanchard*, 2 vols. (London, 1795), I, p. 255.

[15b] PRO TS 11/962/3508.

[16] PRO TS 11/957/3502/1.

[17] PRO TS 11/957/3502/2: 9 May; 'Second Report from the Committee of Secrecy' (6 June 1794) in Sheila Lambert (ed.), *House of Commons Sessional Papers of the Eighteenth Century*, 145 vols. (Wilmington, Delaware, 1975), XCIII, pp. 158–59.

[18] 'The Trial of Thomas Hardy for High Treason', in T. B. and T. J. Howell (compilers), op. cit. (note 7b), XXIV (34 & 35 George III . . . A.D. 1794) (London, 1818), col. 571 (toasts and songs); cols. 750–51 (JHT's speech).

[19] Op. cit. (note 15a), I, pp. 355–57.

[20] All were members of the LCS. Bills were found against Hillier, Francklow, and Spence; but not found against Ashley. Eventually all were released without standing trial, some after lengthy imprisonment. Thomas Spence (1750–1814) was the publisher of the notorious *Pigs' Meat or Lessons for the Swinish Multitude*, a radical journal which ran between 1793 and 1795. Spence's views upon the ultimate wickedness of private property formed a coherent political philosophy which endured after his death. Arthur Thistlewood, hanged for his leadership of the Cato Street Conspiracy in 1820, was a follower of the Spencean philosophy. In 1794–95 Spence was held without trial for seven months.

[21] Meikle, op. cit. (note 13), p. 94.

[22] Meikle, op. cit. (note 13), p. 94.

[23] Meikle, op. cit. (note 13), p. 103; p. 115n.

[24] Sharp's evidence before the Privy Council: PRO PC 2/140 fo. 336 (printed pagination 171).

[25] List of delegates to the joint LCS/SCI Committee of Secrecy (or Correspondence): PRO TS 11/957/3502.

[26] Op. cit. (note 15a), II, p. 227.

[27] Sharp was interrogated before the Privy Council on 24 May, 6 June, and 9 June: PRO PC 2/140.

[28] Taylor's report of his division's LCS meeting of 22 April 1794, in Mary Thale (ed.), *Selections from the Papers of the London Corresponding Society, 1792–1799* (Cambridge, 1983), p. 144.

[29] Sharp on LCS disquiet at SCI: PRO PC 2/140 fo. 340 (printed pagination 173).

[30] Op. cit. (note 17), XCIII, p. 156.

[31] See Walter Sichel (ed.), *The Glenbervie Journals* (London, 1910), pp. 212–13. This is confirmed by the then attorney general, Sir John Scott, who as Lord Eldon later claimed that Eyre's strong opinions expressed in the Privy Council were among the reasons why he prosecuted for high treason rather than sedition: Lord Eldon's *Anecdote Book* quoted in John Lord Campbell, *The Lives of the Lord Chancellors and Keepers of the Great Seal of England, from the Earliest Times till the Reign of*

King George IV, 8 vols. (London, 1845–47, 1869), VII [The life of Lord Eldon], p. 116.

[32] John Lord Campbell, op. cit. (note 31), VII [The life of Lord Eldon], pp. 115–16.

[33] Campbell considered Eldon's arguments unsatisfactory and dismissed the theory of acquittal due to a 'higher' guilt as 'a mere pretext': John Lord Campbell, op. cit (note 31), VII [The life of Lord Eldon], p. 117.

[34] See op. cit. (note 1), pp. 245–53 (Friday 16 May) for Pitt's language in parliament.

[35] PRO PC 2/140.

[36] PRO HO 42/33 quoted in J. Stevenson, 'The London "crimp" riots of 1794', *International Review of Social History*, 16(1971), 40–58, at pp. 48, 51.

[37] Meikle, op. cit. (note 13), pp. 89–90.

[38] PRO PC 2/141.

[39] *The New Annual Register, or General Repository of History, Politics, and Literature, for the Year 1794* (London, 1795), 'British and Foreign History for the Year 1794', p. 269.

[40] See 'Points to be Proved . . . and Names of the Witnesses by whom they are to be proved'. The final 'Point' was the 'Plot to assassinate the King' and the witness named was Thomas John Upton. (PRO TS 11/957/3502/2).

[41] Clive Emsley, 'Repression, "terror" and the rule of law in England during the decade of the French Revolution', *English Historical Review*, 100 (1985), 801–25.

[42] Lord Granville Leveson Gower (first Earl Granville), *Private Correspondence 1781 to 1821*, ed. Castalia, Countess Granville, 2 vols. (London, 1916), I, p. 106.

[43] Sichel (ed.), op. cit. (note 31), pp. 212–14.

[44] John Lord Campbell, *The Lives of the Chief Justices of England from the Norman Conquest till the Death of Lord Tenterden*, 3 vols. (London, 1849, 1857), III (1857), pp. 69–74.

[45] John Lord Campbell, op. cit. (note 44), III (1857), p. 52.

[46] Eyre's speech to the grand jury of the special commission: *The Trial of Mr. Thomas Hardy for High Treason: containing the whole of the proceedings . . . and the bills of indictment found against Thomas Hardy, John Horne Tooke, John Augustus Bonney* [and others] . . . *Accurately taken in short-hand by Manoah Sibley* (Dublin, 1794), p. 18.

[47] [William Godwin], *Cursory Strictures on the Charge delivered by Lord Chief Justice Eyre to the Grand Jury, October 2, 1794* (London, 1794). It is reprinted in T. B. and T. J. Howell (compilers), op. cit. (note 7b), XXIV, where (col. 210) it is ascribed to Felix Vaughan.

[48] 'Addendum to Hardy's Case' in T. B. and T. J. Howell (compilers), op. cit. (note 7b), XXIV, cols. 1399–1402.

[49] Holcroft, op. cit. (note 8), p. 87.

[50] Stephens, op. cit. (note 7a), II, p. 301.

[51] Op. cit. (note 46), pp. 49–50.

[52] Gibbs's speech for the defence: op. cit. (note 15a) II, pp. 161–62.

[53] Hotham to Auckland, 15 November 1794, in William Eden, Baron Auckland, *The Journal and Correspondence of William, Lord Auckland*, ed. G. Hogge, 4 vols. (London, [1860]–62), III, p. 256.

[54] Op. cit. (note 15a), II, pp. 74–75.

[55] Horace Walpole to Hannah More, 21 August 1792, referred to Horne Tooke along with Paine and 'Woolstoncraft' as 'philosophical vipers' in W. S. Lewis (ed.), *Horace Walpole's Correspondence*, 48 vols. (London, New Haven, and Oxford, 1937–83), XXXI, p. 273. See Lord Granville Leveson Gower, op. cit. (note 42), I, p. 105, for his remarks on Horne Tooke at his trial: 'very cool, clever, and witty, at the same time I cannot say his conduct appears in any way disrespectful'.

[56] Brown, op. cit. (note 3), p. 52.

[57] John Horne, *The Petition of an Englishman* (London, 1765), p. 24.

[58] *DNB*, vol. 57, p. 45.

[59] Stephens, op. cit. (note 7a), II, p. 36.

[60] Stephens, op. cit. (note 7a), I, p. 474.

[61] Op. cit. (note 15a), I, p. 354.

[62] John Horne Tooke, *The Diversions of Purley Part I*, 2nd edn. (London, 1798), pp. 74–75.

[63] Lady Bessborough to Lord Granville 27 November 1805: Lord Granville Leveson Gower, op. cit. (note 42), II, pp. 136–38.

[64] Horne Tooke had inflated views as to the value of his philological researches which were to some extent shared in his own day. See Hans Aarslef, *The Study of Language in England, 1780–1860* (Princeton, New Jersey, 1967), c. 2, '*The Diversions of Purley*', and c. 3, 'Horne Tooke's influence and reputation'; see also Olivia Smith, *The Politics of Language, 1791–1819* (Oxford, 1984), c. 4, 'Winged Words: language and liberty in John Horne Tooke's *Diversions of Purley*'.

[65] 'February 18 — The return of Horne Tooke is likely to become one of the first thorns in the side of the new Minister. Is a *priest* eligible? By what tribunal is the question to be tried? He was walking about the House from bench to bench yesterday followed by Sir Francis Burdett. He looks very old and is lame': Francis Bickley (ed.), *The Diaries of Sylvester Douglas (Lord Glenbervie)*, 2 vols. (London, 1928), I, p. 171. See also Lord Granville Leveson Gower, op. cit. (note 42), I, p. 300; and Pitt to George III, 19 February 1801: 'Mr Horne Tooke made a speech which seemed to aim only at quaintness and singularity in its turn, and deserves little remark' in A. Aspinall (ed.), *The Later Correspondence of George III*, 5 vols. (Cambridge, 1962), III, p. 506.

EDITORIAL NOTE

The following editorial conventions have been employed in exposition
of the text of the diary:

{?   }   contains editor's reading of words not clearly legible in the
               original
[   ]   contains, in italics, note by editor
<   >   contains matter crossed out by JHT
>   <   contains JHT's substitution for matter crossed out
«   »   contains matter which is indecipherable
     ↑   indicates the beginning of a superscript insertion by JHT
     ↓   indicates the end of a superscript insertion by JHT
     #   indicates a deliberate editorial omission of matter in original

The spelling (including 'ſs' for 'ss'), punctuation, and paragraphing of
the original have been faithfully reproduced.

The diary is contained between p. 100 and p. 181 of vol. I of a two-
volume interleaved copy of John Horne Tooke's ΕΠΕΑ ΠΤΕΡΟΕΝΤΑ.
OR, THE DIVERSIONS OF PURLEY PART I (London, 1786). In
the present edition page references prefixed by 'p.' in the left margin
refer to the page numbers of the printed text of *The Diversions of
Purley*. Matter originating on these pages is printed here in a smaller
point size. Page references not so prefixed (e.g. 106/07) refer to the
pages of the leaf inserted between two particular numbered pages. The
recto or verso of the leaf is identified by 'r' or 'v'.

Inside the boards at the front of vol. II of this copy of *The Diversions
of Purley* is a tally of Tooke's 191 days in close custody from 16 May
to 22 November 1794 inclusive. Beneath this is written the following:

So far am I from undervaluing kings, that I think they may all be made <use-
ful to> and I earnestly wish they may all be made useful to mankind: the good
by their conduct, and the bad by the example of their destruction.

TEXT OF DIARY

[The following items physically precede the text of the diary. It is more than likely, however, that they were written sometime later, although possibly not much later.]

100/01/v   PAPERS &c.
    In 177<8> >7< I moved to King's Bench prison
    In 1778 I removed to Brentford
    In 1779? I moved to Paper Buildings. Temple
    In 1784? I moved to Whitton near Huntingdon.
          Sarjeants Inn. Rathbone Place.
    In 1788? I moved to Richmond Buildings
    In 1792? June 30. I moved to Wimbledon. Surrey
    1794 to Mefsenger's – To Tower – To Newgate

My things have been moved & removed <u>six</u> times in <u>fifteen</u> years.

      Compositions layed before me
Cartwright, ↑2↓ <u>D.ʳ Vincent</u>. J. {? I.} Adams. Col. Hangar ↑oaths↓
Col. Money. S.ᵗ Cha.ˢ Turner. ↑« » Dunning↓ Beckford. <u>One</u> Loyd.
<u>John Pearson</u>. Thelwall a poem. <u>Harbord Harbord</u>.
Major Jardine. Holcroft. Merry. Addington
the present Speaker. 1788. Batlay senior.
<u>D.ʳ George Pearson</u>.

[Here follows a list of his places of residence.]
    C<u>l</u>are. W<u>est</u>minster. E<u>t</u>on. S<u>ev</u>enoaks.
    <u>R</u>avenstone. C<u>a</u>mbridge. & Temple.
    Blackheath. Downing Street. Cliffe. ↑Cov.ᵗ Garden.↓
    Brentford
    France. Italy. Brentford. Piccadilly. Vine Street
    Serj.ᵗˢ Inn. Purley. H. of Commons. King's Bench
    Paper buildings; Temple ↑Graffham.↓ Whitton. ↑Thorn
    Brampton.↓ Rathbone Place Richmond buildings.
    Wimbledon. King's Mefsenger, Tower. Newgate.
    Wimbledon.

[The following, up to 24 May, was originally written in pencil, and very deliberately written over in ink, presumably after 24 May, when the Privy

Council authorized Horne Tooke to have pen, paper, and ink. See JHT's entry for 24 May.]

102/03/r   I shall certainly die <u>With</u> the principles which I have always profeſsed; and I am very willing to dye <u>For</u> them.

Whilst I live I will support and maintain them by every means within my power. I will resist argument by argument, reason by reason, legal means by legal means, force by force; but every man chuses to take that situation in which he can ↑most↓ advantageously employ his strength; and, as I have never profeſsed any power but reason, I chuse to take the field of argument.

D. of Richmond. Brocklesby. Cartwright. Francis. Wharton.[1]

"I aske after the seete of thy thought, in whiche I put not whylom bookes, but I put that that maketh bookes worthy of pryce or precyous"

1st. boke of Boecius. fol. ccxxiiii.

page 1. col. 2^2.

advertisements of my book and Handbills
refused to be printed
Minors
Jephson
Beadon & A.M., degree & chaplainship
Caldwell. Clitherow. Hardwick.

Wilkes		ald^n. Pickett. G« »
Shelbourne		Harwood
Barre	S^n. Woodfall	Cline
Mazeres		Farrer
Erskine		Baring
Letter to L^d. Ashburton		J. Pearson
(Fox. thanks to Pitt.		Fletcher
(thatched house		F. Vaughan
Trial with Fox		Ld Wycombe

D. Adams Wharton. Thompson . Gawler & brother
W. Sharp   Sinclair.   J. Williams

102/03/v   Sir Rich^d. Pearson   Smith Pitt's Secr^y. [*Altered to* Peer.]
& Michael Pearson
Schomberg Capt.
D. of Athol[3]

Thursday May 15. Dine
at Pearson's[4]. Joyce's letter[5]
May 16. 1794 ↑Friday↓ at noon apprehended by Swift,
Police officer Marlbor[gh] Street
Glitton, Clerk – Thornton Clerk & 3 constables, Kennedy
one of them
at the Treasury at 3.
Nepean's [6] civility.
Reeves[7] must hang me; but wished I might live afterwards.
Privy Council at ½ past 8.
Dundas[8] – "It is <u>conceived</u> etc
"Constitutional & <u>corresponding</u> Societies, of <u>both</u> of which
you are an active and leading member, etc."[9]
My answer, "Refuse to be examined unlefs some
charge."[10]
<u>SAME DAY</u> – Habeas Corpus Bill.[11]
Nepean. Chuse my place of Confinement
Walsh's son[12]

[*Continuing on the same line, but written directly in ink (therefore after
24 May).*]
Richter. ↑H. Tooke & Bonney↓ Thelwall. Joyce. Loveit

[*Continues down right-hand side of the page, again directly in ink.*]
Hardy
Martin
Kyd[13]
Monday May 19. To Tower.
Tuesday 20. Hunter[14] asks me to write to Nepean. Kinghorn
refuses Pen & Ink
Wednesday 21 Newspapers etc forbidden.
Thursday 22 Kinghorn will answer me from Governour
about care of my family.
Friday. He will answer in a few days.
Iron bars put up at the Window.

p. 103 [*Top margin – all directly in ink, so written after 24 May.*]

Privy Council before whom I stood.
Dundas. Grenville Buckingham. Amherst Bayham. Staffordshire. Chancellor and two
others or three others. — Reeves Fawkener Ford, etc.[15]

[*Then down right border.*]   20,000
                              20,000
                               7,000
                              12,000
                               6,000
                               5,000
                              14,000
                              84,000
                              3 others
                              suppose
                              15,000
                              84,000
                              99,000
                              besides
                              extensive
                              influence
                              and patro=
                              =nage to
                              all relations
                              and creatures[16]

104/05/r   American War — King's Bench — £1200
            French War — The Tower
            Friday May 23. Felix Vaughan[17] has order from Privy
            Council to see me in presence of Gaoler. Kinghorn being
            absent, He saw me in presence of Capt. Bruhl[18] of the
            guards in garrison.
            Sat. May 24. I received from Vaughan's ↑servant↓ by order
            of P. Council Pens Ink. Paper. Tea. Sugar. Lozenges for my
            cough
[*From here the diary is written directly in ink.*]
            Lodgings at Burford's[19]
            N.B. Government allows £0. 13. 4 per week Per An.
            £35.2.0[20]
                Warders. 1ˢᵗ week – Burford & Blower.
                Monday May 26: Paid Burford   0. 7.10
                                     Nicholson[21] 3. 3. 7
                                     Barber   0.13. 0
                                     Laundrefs   0. 1. 3½
                                                   4. 5. 8½
            N.B. Governour <u>opened</u> my Child's letter, ↑and sent it
                  <u>open</u> by Kinghorn↓ (Charlotte's). Nepean would not
                  open.

Two new Warders Bouquette & Pearson

F. Vaughan paid me a visit of ½ an hour, Kinghorn's watch in his hand. I gave him my keys. Letter to Zenobia.[22]

↑Ford had examined Lord Hood's £20↓

M.ʳ Ford, the Justice, brought a letter to me from Privy Council, demanding my keys, and he showed me his authority (signed Dundas) for inspecting and taking my books & papers.

M.ʳ Ford told me, he was directed not to take or to trouble himself about sedition or seditious papers, but to confine himself to the discovery of <u>Treason</u>, and especially the Treason of < > < > a <u>Convention</u>.[23]

Tuesday May 27. my apartments changed from Burford's where I had a walk on the wall of 8½ yards by 1½ for the air: and I was escorted by Gentleman Gaoler. 2 Warders in a file of musqueteers, to Mold's house.[24] Burford and Molds both are Warders. I understand all the other prisoners have one Warder; but I have always Two besides the Warder of the house, and a Centinel always at the door.

The two Warders always sit in the same room with me; and always lie all night in the same room with me. I am daily visited twice. i.e. morning and evening by Kinghorn, Gentleman Gaoler, once by the officers of the garrison, and three times by a Serjeant and sometimes four times.

<u>For my Close Stool[25] I had an order from Privy Council.</u> the <u>same for my Snuff</u>. the same for <u>my shirts, stocks, stockings and handkerchiefs</u>

N.B. I learn (from <u>Vaughan</u>) that London Ev.ᵍ Post of tuesday May 27, says – "that the Prisoners in the Tower, have each a Counsel and Solicitor permitted to see them" This falsehood is probably inserted in <u>other papers</u> – N.B. GIBBS[26]

Wednesday May 28. Vaughan visited me the 3.ᵈ time. Kinghorn sat <u>close</u>. He says, he has the Governor's order to hear every syllable that pafses. Vaughan returned me key of my linen drawers: Ford kept key of Book cases etc. and would return them tomorrow. He took away about thirty of my <u>private letters</u>, (amongst which, one to me from <u>Cowper</u>)[27] most of them dated 1792. a Letter signed <u>Regulus</u>[28] etc.

104/05/v

The closet, where Executorship papers,
Sir Rob⁺ Bernard's,[29] & my large travelling

p. 105 [*Bottom margin.*] N.B. Ford did not confine himself to papers of <u>treason</u>: for finding nothing of the kind or about <u>Convention</u>, he took away about thirty insignificant private letters.

106/07/r   trunk, were, was locked up by Ford and the key taken away by M⁺ Ford. – M⁺ Vaughan said M⁺ Ford had dismifsed Thornton (the Police Officer) from my house. So that Constables held pofsefsion of my house & slept there <u>twelve</u> days and eleven nights.

M⁺ Ford said, he would apply to Privy Council that Warder should not sleep in the <u>same</u> room with me.

That I might give Kinghorn something <u>to carry</u> for his listening, I told Vaughan in the broad terms, – that the Ministry might kifs my arse.

This night Kinghorn locked the Warder and me at ten o clock into the Chamber, so that if the warder had had the cholic, he must have shited in the room for my regale. – as had nearly happened to <u>Dixon</u> the warder who attends Thelwall. I rec⁴. ↑government allowance↓ £0.13.4 to May 26. for one week

Thursday May 29. 1794. Warder and I rose at 5 o'clock; but being locked in, could get no fire nor breakfast till seven o'clock.

Friday May 30. 1794. 4ᵗʰ. time F. Vaughan visited me, told me that Frost[30] was taken last night, at my house at Wimbledon, (so that my family are now left defencelefs again: for Frost kindly went there to protect them) J. Williams,[31] the Wine Merchant is taken. Hardy was bro⁺ yesterday to the Tower. Five persons, I know not whom, are sent to Newgate.[32] Privy Council return my keys to Vaughan. By their direction Vaughan offers keys to me. I refuse to touch them, bid him keep them for the present, and take out some title deeds, and my Will, which on

106/07/v   General Murray's[33] death, the Duke of Athol had caused M⁺ Squire to return to me. Kinghorn, when Vaughan was going, interfered about my keys, which he wanted Vaughan to deliver to him. Said, he had been reported ↑ & blamed ↓

for suffering <him> >Vaughan< to receive them before. – acknowledges he had not been <u>reported</u>, but had mentioned it himself.

This Kinghorn is <u>gaoler</u>, but not <u>Gentleman Gaoler</u>. He has uniformly given me <u>fawning</u> words, and most <u>savage</u> treatment. Vaughan says, Mr Ford would obtain from Privy Council to remove Warder from sleeping in my room, but wished I would apply.

N.B. <u>My confinement in King's Bench</u>[34] <u>ruined my Boy.</u> <u>God send that the Tower produces no future mischief to my</u> <u>Girls.</u>[35] Before my apprehension by Dundas's warrant, I had slept out of my house but one night (at Margate) for the last seven years. Vaughan retained Gibbs for me yesterday. (The governour sent me yesterday a handsome letter from a Mr Dowse (whom I do not know) of Warwick Court, requesting my vote for a Mrs Leavey to be matron of the Asylum)[36]

Saturday <June> >May< 31. Iron bars put up at Window, the 2^d time of performing ceremony.[37] Martin, the Attorney[38] bro! to the Tower: put in a miserable apartment at Jackson's, the Warder, a relation of Kinghorn's?

At ten o'clock this night, Kinghorn says, he has just received order to remove the Warders bed into adjoining room.

Sunday, June.1. 1794.

Warder's bed removed to adjoining room. I walked upon the Leads, twice for 20 minutes each time, attended by two Warders and a Centinel with bayonet fixed, <both> 1st time whilst my bed was turned up and the room swept; The 2^d time whilst my bed was making for night.

p. 108 [*Bottom margin.*]

1794	
May 23	5. 5. 0
June 2	20. 0. 0
Wildman	10. 0. 0
Dr Pearson	20. 0. 0
July 7	
Mr Cline	20. 0. 0
	75. 5. 0

108/09/r   Monday. June 2 1794.
This morning at six o'clock, The Yeoman Porter, (a natu-
ralised Frenchman or Swiſs, who had been a servant of
Lord Shipbrook, General Vernon's brother, the ↑L:↓ governour of the Tower)[39] found great fault with Bouquet, the
Warder, for permitting me to walk upon the Leads.
N.B. I have <u>now</u> been, <u>this day at noon</u>, seventeen days &
nights in <u>Close</u> custody; without any hint or conjecture
what action or crime can be laid to my charge.
I recᵈ for 2ᵈ week 0.13.4. government maintenance of a
prisoner; So that they have at last found out a method to
make me a <u>pensioner</u> against my will.
F. Vaughan visited me ↑ 5ᵗʰ time↓. He had received from
H. ᴸᴸ £50. He gave me £20. and will give to Wildman[40] to
pay to Mrs Hart[41] £10 due to her the
1ˢᵗ May 1794. £50

                  5. 5. rec   from V. before
                 44.15.0
                 30. 0.0   Self & Hart
     Remain   14.15.0

He is to pay for my hat; & he has retained Gibbs.

I have in pocket	gold	12. 1. 6
	silver	0.12. 6
	bank note	10. 0. 0
		22.14. 0

N.B. Mr Tooke[42] gave my girls £10.10.0 May 24.
Two new Warders   Finney . Lᵈ Cornwallis's[43] servant
                  Lockit . Abp. Cornwallis's[44] cook.

Tuesday June 3 1794

Half a pound of Snuff sent by Mr Vaughan, was turned out
of the paper and examined by Kinghorn. At noon
Kinghorn broᵗ a halfsieve[45] sent by my girls, with goose-ber-
ries, pease, strawberries. It was opened, and in it was a
108/09/v   Letter from Charlotte, which Kinghorn took to carry to the
governour Mr Yorke.[46] At ten at night (for I staid up to
read it) Kinghorn brought it back to me, <u>open</u> (N.B. This is
the second time the governor has opened and read my girls'
letter, and sent them back to me <u>open</u>, so that Gaoler, & if

he pleased, the whole garrison might read them – a very little delicacy or even reflection would teach a governour (if he did break open letters from a prisoner's family) at least to inclose them in a note sealed from himself, that the prisoner might know his private affairs were open only to the governor himself and not to every fellow.)

I had permifsion to send some strawberries by one of the Warders to Bonney.

Wednesday. June 4. 1794. The Bells are ringing for the King's Birthday.

I get in this place between 7 and 8 hours reading and writing each day; so that I do not get any advantage in that respect by my confinement.

A Lock with great formality ↑put↓ on outer door.

Thursday. June 5. 1794

A Man with a Pea-cart stands ↑this moment↓ under my window drawn by an afs: the afs began to bray. the master seized him by the snout and began to belabour him unmercifully to stop his braying, to the scandal of the private soldiers, who interfered humanely with the man, to suffer his afs to bray without molestation and cruelty. – These soldiers have me (as patient and as industrious as the afs) in custody for braying.

A corporal and a Serjeant come in to my room, two of them, every two hours and sometimes each hour, besides two Warders in my room, a centinel at the door and another

110/11/r on the staircase: if they kept out of room and kept a thousand round it it would be lefs unpleasant: for they chuse often to rush suddenly into my room; which the other Warders, Burford, & Blower and Bouquet and Pearson, used to prevent.

Friday. June 6. 1794.

Kinghorn brought my keys. and some brown paper from Privy Council; and told me that M⁻ Vaughan had been examined by Privy Council,[47] and was forbid to visit me any more till further order; he said M⁻ Hague[48] was also forbidden to visit M⁻ Bonney; (I did not before know that Hague did visit him) Privy Council, he said, permitted me newspapers, and to walk upon the Leads.

(2 Warders and a Centinel; bayonet fix'd & another
Centinel on staircase)
I have this day at noon been 3 weeks in CLOSE custody.
N.B. F. Vaughan has visited me five times, half an hour
each time; in all two hours and a half, Kinghorn sitting
close by my side, and chusing to mix in the conversation,
and from time to time looking at his watch, to see when the
half hour should expire. At the last visit Vaughan said, he
expected to be examined, and should of course visit me
immediately afterwards. He is <u>forbid to visit me any more</u>.[49]

p. 110 [*Top margin.*] F. Vaughan had visited me Five times; half an hour each time,
the Gaoler sitting close to hear every syllable, with his watch in his hand; and often
joining (without invitation) in the conversation So that I had Vaughan's company,
under these circumstances, <   > <u>Two hours</u> and a <u>half</u> in all.

110/11/r   I received a basket with lemons, strawberries etc. and a let-
(continued) ter from Charlotte, which <u>Kinghorn</u> read. I had <u>his</u> permiſ-
             sion to send some strawberries and artichokes to Bonney.
             This day I had for the first time. Chronicle, Post, Gazetteer,
             World, Herald, Oracle, Times, True Briton, and two Eveng
             papers – Courier, Star.[50] – I sent them to Warder, Bouquet,
             for use of such prisoners as were <u>allowed</u> to read them.
             Saturday June 7. 1794
             Corresponding Society's Advertisement in the Morning
             Post.[51] The visiting Officer of the Guard asked me very
             politely, if I had in my apartment every thing I
110/11/v   wanted? – yes, Sir, <u>All</u>, and <u>more</u> than I want, by two
             Warders, two Centinels, and all the bolts and Bars. –
             Two o'clock Rofs the Meſsenger, tells me, he ↑with
             Higgins,↓[52] has just bro! Kyd to the Tower. Kyd is at the
             Warder Lockit's. Sharp[53] is still in custody at his own
             house. Frost is on honour to return to Privy Council on
             monday.
             Hull[54] has given Security to appear the first day of term.
             Privy Council are to make a general arrangement for all the
             prisoners, that their friends may have accefs to them etc etc.
             Kyd agrees with Lockit, as Joyce with Dixon eighteen pence
             for dinner. They find every thing else for themselves.
             Rofs, the Meſsenger asked Kinghorn's permiſsion to see me:
             Kinghorn refused.[55]

Sunday. June 8. 1794

In last night's Courier, is the act of Parl! "To empower his <u>Majesty</u> (i.e. the <u>Minister</u>) to ↑«*Two or three words crossed out and illegible.*»↓ secure and detain (i.e. To ↑<u>rob</u>↓ <u>ruin</u> and <u>murder</u>*)

p. 111 [*Bottom margin. JHT's own asterisked note.*](*) I call it <u>murder</u>; because in<u>defin</u>ite and ar<u>bitrary</u> imprisonment, CLOSE CUSTODY (such as I experience) with all its circumstances of <u>time</u> and <u>place</u> and <u>manner</u> at the <u>will</u> of a <u>malicious</u> minister, may be, certain death by the slow torture of disease.

110/11/v   such persons as his <u>Majesty</u> (i.e. the <u>Minister</u>) shall <u>suspect</u>
(continued) (i.e. <u>pretend</u> to suspect) are conspiring against his person and government. (i.e. Who are displeased with the minister's measures or to whom the minister is, for any reason, ↑or misinformat^n or mistake, or caprice↓ hostile.) The Act <u>afsumes</u> that – "A traitorous and detestable conspiracy has been formed for subverting the existing Laws and constitution, and for introducing the system of anarchy and confusion which has so fatally prevailed in France; <u>Therefore</u> (N.B. Remember that, the foundation of this <u>Therefore</u> is <u>suddenly</u> <u>afsumed</u> without a hearing or any proof) "for the better preservation of his Majesty's {*?* sacred} person, and for <u>securing</u> the peace.[56]

p. 112 [*Bottom half of page: an attempt by JHT to construct the roster of warders attending him.*]

Tower
1794
Monday. May 19. <u>Burford</u>. Blower
Monday. May 26. Bouquet. Pearson
Monday. June. 2. <u>Finney</u>. <u>Lockhead</u>.
Monday. June. 9. Jackson. Bateman
Monday, June. 16. <u>Underwood</u>
Monday. June. 23. <u>Wallace</u>
Friday. June 27. Newman.
Monday. July. 7. <u>Dixon</u>
Monday. July. 14. <u>Warner</u>
Monday July 21. Pearson 2^d time
Monday. July. 28. · <u>Mould</u>. [*Underlining cancelled with a wavy line.*]
Monday Augst 4. Jackson 2^d time
Monday Augst 11. Newman 2^d time
Monday Aug. 18. <u>Cooper</u>. [*Underlining cancelled with wavy line.*]

Monday Aug. 25. Newman 3ᵈ. time
Monday Sept 1 <u>Perry</u>
Monday Sept. 8. Bouquet 2ᵈ. time
Monday Sept. 15. <u>Dobson</u>
Monday Sept. 22. Blower 2ᵈ. time
Monday Sept. 29. Bateman 2ᵈ. time
Monday Oct. 6 Mould 2ᵈ. time
               13 Cooper 2ᵈ. time
               20 Newman 4ᵗʰ. time

[*No leaf inserted between p. 112 and p. 113 of* DoP.]
p. 114 [*Top, left, and bottom margins: continuation of JHT's roster of warders attending him.*]

1 Monday	<u>Yorke</u>. Governour	Officers
Burford. May. 19	<u>Kinghorn</u>. Gaoler	Bruhl
Blower. 1794	<u>Brice</u>. Adjutant	Buckley
2 May 26.		

Bouquet
Pearson
     3 June 2.
Finney.
Lockhead
     4 June 9.
<u>Jackson</u>
<u>Bateman</u>   Perry. Dobson. Hemings.
     5ᵗʰ. week   Cooper
     June. 16.   [Louis Gruaz]
Underwood 9ᵗʰ.   Gr↑u↓az. yeoman Porter.
     6ᵗʰ. week
     commencing
     June 23.
Wallace. 10ᵗʰ.
Friday June 27
Newman
     11ᵗʰ.
8ᵗʰ Monday
     July 7. 1794
Dixon. 12th
9ᵗʰ Monday.
     July. 14 1794
     Warner. 13ᵗʰ.
10ᵗʰ July 21.
     Pearson
     a 2ᵈ. time.
11ᵗʰ. July. 28.
     Mould 14ᵗʰ. [*The name deleted.*]

Jackson [*The named deleted and virtually illegible.*]

12ᵗʰ. Augˢᵗ. 4.	Burford	<u>Blower</u>
Jackson	<u>Bouquet.</u>	Lockit
2ᵈ time	Underwood.	<u>Wallace</u>
13ᵗʰ. Augˢᵗ. 11.	Newman.	<u>Warner</u>
Newman	[*Final name deleted and*	
14. Augˢᵗ. 18	*illegible.*]	
Cooper		

p. 115 [*Top, left, and right margins: continuation of JHT's roster of warders attending him.*]

<u>Burford</u>. <u>Blower</u>. <u>Bouquet</u>. <u>Pearson</u>.
<u>Tinney</u>. <u>Lockhead</u>. Jackson. Bateman.
<u>Underwood</u>. Wallace. <u>Newman</u>. Dixon
Warner. Mould. Cooper. Perry. Dobson.

Week
15ᵗʰ. Augˢᵗ. 25
   Newman
16ᵗʰ. Septʳ. 1.
   Perry
17ᵗʰ Septʳ.   8
   Bouquet
18ᵗʰ. Septʳ. 15
   Dobson
19ᵗʰ. Septʳ. 22
   Blower
20ᵗʰ Septʳ. 29
   Bateman
21 October 6
   ·Mould
22 Octʳ. 13
   Cooper
23 Octʳ. 20
   Newman

114/15/r   Monday June 9. 1794

I saw Joyce upon <a> ↑top of a↓ distant house Leads.
We bowed to each other.
I saw Kyd upon the Leads, we bowed to each other.
N.B. I understand (by an accident) that Vaughan was prohibited from seeing me any more, because he excused himself (as Counsel for four of the prisoners) from being examined by Privy Council[57]
A basket from Wimbledon from my gardener. It must not be opened till Kinghorn comes, who will read my girl's letter; and then, if he approves the contents, will graciously communicate them to me: after which he will perhaps permit me to send some strawberries to Mʳ Bonney.

At nine o'clock this morning, two new Warders came. Bateman and Jackson. I understand their <u>characters</u> and <u>disposition</u>; and am not at all pleased to be in their hands. Pazienza! My custody cannot easily be <u>closer</u>; though it may be made more disagreable by their presence and conduct.

I <u>wrote</u> to M.ʳ Fawkener, Clerk of Privy Council. {?Please give} permifsion for D.ʳ Pearson my physician and M.ʳ Cline, my surgeon,[58] to attend me.

(For this letter – See 4 pages forward) [*i.e.,* *118/19ʳ⁻ᵛ*]

N.B. Privy Council wanted Vaughan to prove my hand writing (or what they supposed so) in some alterations or amendments in some resolutions of Constit. Society. He refused to be examined on the subject. They told him that as he was my intimate friend he was wrong to refuse: it <u>might cause me to be confined the longer</u> !![59]

114/15/v   Tuesday June. 10. 1794

I read in the <u>Times</u> "the second Report of secret Committee of House of Lords."[60]

I immediately wrote the following letter to M.ʳ Fawkener and sent it off before Dinner; though the newspaper did not come to me <u>this</u> day till eleven o'clock: and the Times was the 8.ᵗʰ <u>Paper</u> I read.

   "Sir

"I request you to represent to the Lords of the Privy Council, in my name; that, having been but very recently permitted to see the newspapers, I have only this moment read, in a paper called The Times, what is entitled – "The second Report from the Committee of Secrecy, appointed by the House of Lords." –

   The first Report I have never seen.

I beg you, Sir, to recall to their lordships' memory, that I was apprehended on the 16ᵗʰ of May, by a warrant of M.ʳ Dundas, directing me "for treasonable practices, to be brought before his presence." At the same time my papers were seized, and my house taken pofsefsion of by several constables without Warrant.

When I was brought before the Privy Council, I was only told by M.ʳ Dundas, that – "<u>It was conceived</u> that I was a member, and an <u>active and leading</u> member of the

Corresponding Society and of the society for Constitutional Information; and that I had; in conjunction with those societies, been guilty of treasonable practices; and that I was therefore apprehended, and brought to the Privy Council to be examined."

Although this was a grofs misconception in every part of it; and of which, I suppose, I could in a few minutes have satisfied their lordships; yet, being an Englishman, acquainted

116/17/r with the laws of my country, to the best of my understanding always governed in my actions not only by the spirit but by the letter of them, yielding implicit obedience to them, and (as I imagined) protected by them; I thought it my duty not to submit to a proceeding which was (at that time) illegal. I therefore refused to be examined. But even this refusal was not (as it might justifiably have been) absolute, but conditional: For I know (and I think it fitting) that, upon extraordinary occasions (or such as are fairly and reasonably thought so) the government of a country may meritoriously depart from the letter of the law, for the safety and security of the country. I therefore declared myself "willing and ready to be examined to any extent, and to give a direct and clear answer to any question put to me, provided the Lord Chancellor or M.ʳ Dundas would declare to me, that there was <u>any</u> Information upon oath against me for <u>Any</u> treason whatever."[61]

Nothing can more effectually confirm the propriety of my refusal (if it wanted confirmation) than the Act of parliament, which has since been pafsed, to authorize the Secretary of State to detain, in <u>SAFE</u> custody, upon <u>suspicion</u>.[62]

My situation therefore is now altered in this country – I am, <u>By Law</u>, at the mercy of Suspicion. With the old methods of proceeding I was a little acquainted: but by what rules or forms <u>Suspicion</u> is to be encountered, I am totally ignorant. – But it is now the LAW. – I deplore it – and submit to it.

116/17/v I have been in the closest pofsible custody now near a month, without being able to form even a conjecture concerning what sort of <u>treasonable</u> practices I could be suspected. I have, this moment only, read that Report of

Horrour: and by that alone am informed, what sort of a picture their lordships have drawn of me in their imagination, and (by their commitment of me to the Tower) have exhibited of me to the world.

My objections to examination by the Privy Council are now intirely removed. Their proceedings are now made legal by the act of Parliament: and the nature of their suspicions are declared.

Such suspicions are too horrid for me to remain under, a moment, in <u>voluntary</u> silence. My character is worth much more than my life. I am anxious to be examined. To shrink from any examination, under such monstrous charges, would appear to me like guilt. And I hope their lordships will think their justice concerned to hear me. And let them afterwards do their pleasure."

I am, Sir, your most

Tower   obedient servant.

June<9>↑10↓.1794   John Horne Tooke"

M⌃ Fawkener

Clerk of the Privy Council

118/19/r   I received an answer from M⌃ Fawkener verbally, by Kinghorn, that the Privy Council did not sit this day; but would sit on Wednesday.

Copy of the letter which I wrote to M⌃

Fawkener on Monday June 9. 1794

   Sir

      Being in such close custody as to have not the smallest communication with any human being, since the permifsion of seeing M⌃ Vaughan has been rescinded; I applied this morning (through the gaoler) to the Governour; that M⌃ Cline of Guy's hospital, my surgeon, and Doctor George Pearson, of S⌃ George's hospital, my physician, might be permitted to see me, at any time convenient to them, so as not to interfere with their other practice.

      The Governour (through the Gaoler) informs me, that he is not the proper channel through which my application should be made; but that I must apply to you.

In consequence of this information, I give you the present trouble. And as my private affairs have been all laid open to the Privy Council; I feel no great repugnance to lay open

to them my more private bodily infirmities, which their
<u>Warrant now reaches by consequence</u>.

I have a dropsy, or a rupture, or both, or a Schirrus[63] in
the testicles, besides a more painful complaint in their
neighbourhood; for which, as well as for swelling in my legs
and other unpleasant symptoms, I have long had the benefit
of their afsistance. This state of my health drove me to
Wimbledon, where I appeared to be recovering. My present
situation has increased my complaints, and I wish for their
advice. I ask that their attendance may be made convenient

118/19/v to themselves: because neither Counsel, nor physicians, nor
surgeons, have ever taken fees from me; and I had rather
lose the benefit of their afsistance, than put them to extraordinary inconvenience, however chearfully they might perhaps submit to it, under my present circumstances.

I am Sir, with respect
your most obedient servant
John Horne Tooke

Tower
June 9. 1794
M.r Fawkener

Thursday June 12. 1794
I read this day in the Herald, the first part of the <u>Second</u>
report of the Committee of House of Commons. I have not
yet received any answer to my application to be examined.
Friday June. 13. 1794 ↑N.B. A month in↓ <u>close</u> custody.
I understand that M.r John Williams (thro' the interest of
Gen.l Archer or Col. Archer, his wife's father or brother)
has been admitted to bail £500. – The difficulty about him
arose from his refusing to swear, that some paper which
they showed him was the hand writing of J. Horne Tooke.
They asked, "Had he ever seen me write. He had. Was this
of my Hand-writing. He could not say it was."[64]
– I understand also that Martin's Clerk,[65] after repeated

120/21/r examinations, is expected to be committed to Newgate, this
day, because he persists in declaring "that he knows nothing
of his master's affairs or actions, but his businefs as an
attorney, his master having never employed him nor dis-
coursed with him about any thing else."

N.B. About 7 o'clock in the evening. the Warder Dixon,

and M[r]. Kyd, were walking upon the Leads (about the size
of my room) under my window. I was standing at the <u>open</u>
window, (for it was very hot) taking snuff. The Warder
asked me for some snuff. I put a little in a piece of coarse
paper and threw it to him. He thanked me, and said, he
hoped he should one day drink a glafs of wine with me,
when I was out of the Tower. I answered, that I should
drink it with him with pleasure: for I supposed he was a
man about my own age. He said, No. He was ten years
younger. How so? said I. Why, what age are you? He said,
this day was his Birthday: and he was this day exactly fifty.
Oh! answered I, if this is your birthday, I will certainly
drink a glafs of wine to your health. I opened a bottle,
filled a glafs, showed it at the window, and drank to his
health. I then said, tho' we are at a distance from each
other, we may still drink together: for if I might I could let
down the bottle with a string. He said, aye, do so. – I tied a
string to the neck of the bottle, and let it down. He got a
glafs, filled it, and drank to my health. I drew the bottle
back. But I never exchanged a single word with M[r]. Kyd.

120/21/v   This was done openly, in sight of the opposite Centinel. A
great piece of work has been made of this.[66]
"Seldom that the steel'd Jayler is the Friend of Man."[67] All
the way through, well exemplified in the Tower.
SATURDAY. June 14
    I see in Papers <u>Addrefs</u> proposed by Lord Grenville in
House of Lords.[68] – and Secretary <u>Dundas with Chief Justice
Eyre</u>[69] <u>have audience of King</u>.
At three o'clock, Kinghorn came to me on the Leads called
the Warder, Jackson, and blamed him for suffering me to
talk to M[r]. Kyd: he said the <u>Adjutant Brice</u>,[70] had made a
<u>Report</u> to the Governour. I told Kinghorn the fact as it
pafsed.
N.B. This Adjutant <u>Brice</u>, I am told, went a day or two ago
in to M[r]. Joyce's room and insulted him and abused Lord
Stanhope[71] to him. This is ↑the↓ son of M[r]. <u>Brice</u> in
Newman Street, who married, lately Mifs —— and whom I
have seen at M[r]. Gahagan's, and with whose sister, my girls
were intimate.
N.B. <u>Jackson</u> proposed that I should not go near my win-

dow. <u>Bateman</u>, on this hot day, shut the window; but I denied his authority and opened it.

SUNDAY. June 15.

I receive this morning, by the Gaoler, the following note, <u>OPEN</u>. (All the other notes from Mr Fawkener were sealed.)

"Council Office Whitehall

14 June 1794

"Sir

"I duly received your letter dated Tower June 10. 1794; and having taken the earliest opportunity of laying the same before the Lords of his majesty's most honourable Privy Council, I am to acquaint you that I have nothing in command from their Lordships on the subject thereof."

I am, Sir, your most obedient

humble Servant

"W. Fawkener"

Mr John Horne Tooke, <u>Clerk</u>

122/23/r N.B. I desired Kinghorn to give me any directions he pleased for my conduct whilst in his custody. He said, he did not know that I needed any; and that he had told the Governour so.

MONDAY. June 16. 1794. N.B. A month in <u>Close</u> custody in the <u>Tower</u>.

<u>Jackson</u> tells me that the Governour has ordered that henceforward, I am to have only <u>ONE</u> Warder to attend me. Kinghorn tells me, that I shall have only ONE Warder; that he told the Governour <u>One</u> was enough. Trinity Brethren⁷² have ↑a↓ procefsion, and go to Deptford from the Tower, and back again, Dine afterwards at London Tavern.

<u>UNDERWOOD</u> – the new Warder this week.

I read Mr Thompson's examination⁷³ in the Morning Post. I received £0. 13. 4 from Kinghorn at ½ past three. Dr Pearson and Mr Cline paid me a visit together. Kinghorn coming with them and sitting close to hear my complaints and their words in answer. I desired them both to observe what sort of custody I was in; I added to Mr Cline, unbuttoning my breeches, "and now Sir, I suppose the Gaoler will likewise chuse to handle my Cods⁷⁴ too with you, of

which he is undoubtedly the master to do his pleasure."
Kinghorn, upon this <u>coarse</u> speech, had just the modesty to
rise from his chair and go to the door in the <u>ante-room</u>. In
two minutes Kinghorn returned. D.ʳ Pearson would then
have given me two ten pound Bank notes which M.ʳ
Vaughan had sent me (being the remainder of the £50) but
M.ʳ Kinghorn took them, examined them and gave them to
me. I desired Pearson and Cline to see my girls, to conceal
from them my treatment, and my health, and to desire them
to send me some fruit.

122/23/v Tuesday. June 17.
M.ʳ Cline paid me a visit, about 5 o'clock. Kinghorn told
me that Felix Vaughan had called on him to inquire after
my health. He told me too that Hague, Bonney's brother in
Law, (who was at first permitted to visit Bonney) had been
forbidden to visit Bonney at the same time that Vaughan
had been forbidden to visit me.

Wednesday June 18. 1794

Kinghorn brought me a Pores injection[75] from D.ʳ Pearson.
D.ʳ Pearson paid me a visit.
Insulted by a serjeant.
M.ʳ Cline paid me a {?visit}: & Kinghorn, withdrew very
civilly.
M.ʳ Weston declines being my attorney. Respects and loves
me. Is anxious to be employed on the occasion; but has
married M.ʳ Styles's (Commiſs.ʳ of Customs) daughter, and
does not dare to be employed.
Changed my broken buckles for new pair from Hemings.
Bond street

Thursday June 19. 1794.

An in<u>famous song</u> in the <u>True Briton</u>.
An insolent soldier– (the second time) { the first
time, a
<u>handkerchief.</u>[76]

M.ʳ Cline paid me a visit ½ past seven.
N.B. He was obliged to wait an hour and a half before he
could see me. He will apply to M.ʳ Nepean.

FRIDAY . June 20. 1794.

I have this ↑day↓ been <u>Five</u> weeks in <u>Close</u> Custody.
I walked only half an hour, for the same reason (this is the

third time) M.ʳ Cline has seen Nepean, thinks him not friendly. paid me a visit.

House of Commons adjourned till Monday June 30.

SATURDAY . June 21. 1794

Overslept myself a full hour, did not rise till 7.

Sent fruit & vegetables to <u>all</u> the prisoners & to K.

M.ʳ Cline paſsed a bougie[77] and left me some to use myself. X

124/25/r

SUNDAY. June 22. 1794.

M.ʳ Pitt at Privy Council, quarrelled last week with Will. Sharp. Sharp words paſsed on both sides.

Reeves said – "Well, we can do without his evidence, Let him be sent to prison and hanged with the rest of them in the Tower" – M.ʳ Pitt ordered him to be sent to the Tower. Lord Grenville opposed it.[78]

MONDAY June 23. 1794

Received from government £0. 13. 4

M.ʳ Cline paſsed a Bougie. X

Wallace the new Warder, who attends me this week.

TUESDAY. June 24. 1794

Arthur Blake's advertisement in Morning Chronicle.[79] Honest.

Some fruit, as usual, to Prisoners & to K.

Paid my bill to M.ʳˢ Mould to this day ↑exclusive↓ £1.6.8.

WEDNESDAY. June 25. 1794

"NOVICE JOHN" in the Morning Post,[80] is a <u>masterpiece indeed</u>. – It is a proof <u>to me</u> that Truth, in this country, will triumph: no villainy nor slaughter can extinguish it. and whatever may at any time befall me, Bleſsed be God for the principles which have unceasingly actuated my mind & conduct.

Adjutant Brice paid me a long visit, and was very civil and perfectly well-behaved.

THURSDAY. June 26. 1794

D.ʳ Pearson paid me a visit

FRIDAY. June 27. 1794

Kinghorn bro.ᵗ me a Letter from Blake attorney in Eſsex street, reminding me that my note for 207.10.ˢ became due. Kinghorn tells me that the Governor has a letter for me from Melton Mowbray which he cannot read, and therefore shall carry to the Privy Council. I never knew any one

124/25/v   [*This page is taken up with a long quotation from Pierre Poivre's* Voyages d'un Philosophe *(London, 1768), p. 44, describing the misery of the arbitrary tyranny suffered by the people of Siam. This is part of his editorial work for the second edition of* DoP; *but scrawled underneath it, perhaps while he was in the Tower, but possibly at a later period when he was inveighing against the evils of the income tax, is the following remark:*]
Happy, happy England, if every thy ↑miserable↓ inhabitants shall, in respect of taxation, be elevated to the condition of the Siamois; <and that> >when< thy Task-masters shall be contented with half the produce of thy industry!
The whole of the quotation appears on p. 89 of the 2nd edn. of DoP (*1798*).]

126/27/r   at or near Melton Mowbray; and have no correspondents any where in the World. What therefore this can mean it is impofsible for me to conjecture. Perhaps the beginning of some scheme against me by Mefs.ʳˢ Reeves and his employers.[81] I fear them not: and trust without the smallest doubt, that falsehood of every kind will, from its nature, furnish ample means for its own detection.
General Vernon, the Governour,[82] came into the Tower, and appointed the Warder, Wallace, to afsist Kinghorn, instead of the Serjeant Hilton, in attending those who are permitted to see the Prisoners.

The Warder, Newman, attends me ↑the remainder of↓ this week, instead of Wallace.
Mʳ. Cline visited me. (6 weeks in Close Custody)
                SATURDAY . June. 28. 1794
Sent fruit & vegetables, as I do daily, to every prisoner.
Mʳ. Cline pafsed bougie. X.
                Sunday June 29.
N.B. About a week ago. Dundas's Son and Nephew, William, chosen to Parliament.[83]
                Monday June 30. 1794.
Received my pension 13 shillings & four pence.
  I have now been 6 weeks in the Tower.
                Tuesday July 1. 1794

Wednesday July. 2. 1794

M.ʳ Cline paid me a visit.

Paid Nicholson 2.18.11 in full to June 30 inclusive.

M.ʳ Wood the special pleader, is employed by the Attorney General to draw Indictment.[84]

126/27/v

Thursday July. 3. 1794.

D.ʳ Pearson attended me, with M.ʳ Cline and M.ʳ Keate,[85] in consultation on my case.

Kyd. 37 years old this day.

Friday. July 4. 1794

I have been (this day) seven weeks in <u>Close</u> Custody, without any charge or accusation. and all that I know or can conjecture of the cause which is to be pretended, is; that M.ʳ Dundas told me "It was <u>conceived</u>" (he would not say by <u>Whom</u> or <u>Why</u>) "that I was an active and leading member of the <u>Corresponding</u> and Constitutional societies; and had been guilty of treasonable practices." Sent fruit & vegetables to each of the prisoners, as I have done, every day. i.e. To Bonney. Kyd, Joyce, Martin, Richter, Hardy, Thelwal. Loveit.

Saturday. July 5. 1794

I rose at half past three. M.ʳ Cline visited me. Kinghorn at night, broᵗ me a meſsage from Bonney: "that he had some intelligence from M.ʳˢ Bonney that the trials were to come on immediately, by the special order of the king, who was eager for them."

I believe, I am 58 years old, this day.

Sunday July 6. 1794

I understand that Kyd and Joyce have authority for saying that we shall all be out of the tower this week: that Wood tells the Attorney General it is impoſsible to indict for treason, and therefore advises him to file an information.[86]

Monday July . 7. 1794 Dixon the Warder

7 weeks in the Tower. M.ʳ Cline visited me. I received my weekly pension of £0. 13. 4.

Tuesday July 8. 1794.

I received yesterday by hands of M.ʳ Cline £20

Received before   5.   5
   from {?T}   20
   for Hart   10
   from V. by C.   20
                                                      75.   5

I have this day   38. 15.   6
                         36. 9.   6

Tower Pension   4. 13.   4
75.   5   41. 2. 10
  4. 13.   4
  5.   1.   8
85.   0.   0

(my expenses are at least 7 pounds or guineas per week.)

p. 127   # [*Some rather inaccurate financial calculations.*]

128/29/r   Wednesday July. 9. 1794
Mʳ Cline visited me. The Allies quit Flanders.[87]
In 1777. After I had been in the King's bench about
7 weeks<,> (I believe) Genˡ. Burgoyne was captured at
Saratoga: (i.e. the news of it reached us).
When I had been 7 weeks in the tower, the allied army
retired from Flanders and Brabant !!!
                          Thursday. July 10. 1794
Sent vegetables, <u>Pie</u>. fruit etc to each prisoner as usual.

p. 128 [*Top margin.*]
    a Pie to Bonney
    D° – to Martin & Loveit
    D° – to Hardy & Thelwall
    D° – to Bonney

128/29/r   FRIDAY. July. 11. 1794
(continued) I have been this day <u>eight</u> weeks in <u>CLOSE</u> custody; and
cannot yet even <u>conjecture</u> what will be laid to my
charge. – Joyce says, our trials are not to come on till
<u>september</u>.
Mʳ Cline paid me a visit.
                          SATURDAY. July 12. 1794
King's speech of yesterday !!!
Walker's trial.[88]

Sunday. July. 13. 1794   🖋   For D.ʳ

Beattie.[89]

"Don Hannibal de Chinchilla. He was a man of 60. Besides his having but one leg and but one arm, he had one eye covered with a piece of green taffeta, and his face seemed slashed in several places. He told me in what engagements he had lost an eye at Naples; an arm in Lombardy; and a leg in the Low countries. What I admired in all the accounts he gave me of his battles and sieges, was<,> that he did not let slip one vain-glorious exprefsion, not one word in his own praise; Though I <u>could willingly have for-given his bragging of that half of him which was left,</u> <u>to make him amends for the lofs of the other.</u>" Gil Blas. Vol. 3 Book vii. chap. xii

"You see by this, that <u>the other half of me is still in arrears to my country</u>; and that I am very likely to <u>return</u> as I came."[90]

128/29/v   Monday July 14. 1794

I have this day been 8 weeks in CLOSE custody in the Tower. Yesterday was suffocatingly hot. I read ↑this day↓ in all the papers – "yesterday M.ʳ Pitt with a party of his friends, dined with several members of both houses of parliament, at M.ʳ Dundas's villa at Wimbledon." — The air no doubt blows fresher on them, from the consideration, that his next door neighbour was sent to spend his summer a close prisoner in the Tower; and they might contemplate with luxury the forlorn condition of my poor disconsolate girls.[91]

"For thee, fair freedom, welcome all the past"[92]

———

Received £0. 13. 4. my pension from government. M.ʳˢ Saunders of the Tower gave my hairdrefser a shilling to drink my health.

M.ʳ Cline paid me a visit.

Tuesday July.15. 1794

M.ʳ Kinghorn tells me that the <u>Sheriff</u> of London (who is <u>paviour to the Tower</u>)[93] declares that all the prisoners in the Tower are to be arraigned for High-treason on Friday.

Wednesday. July. 16. 1794

Mʳ Cline paid me a visit.

THURSDAY. July 17. 1794

───────

FRIDAY. July.18.1794

This day, I have been 9 weeks in CLOSE custody.

Mʳ Cline paid me a visit

SATURDAY July 19. 1794

Mʳ Cline came

Sunday July 20. 1794

Walking about my room, I accidentally stopped for a minute looking out of my window at a boat on the Thames. The wharf was full of people, and to my surprize, they all together suddenly pulled off their hats to me; this

p. 130   # [*List, apparently of persons owed money.*]

130/31/r   # [*More financial calculations.*]

130/31/v   is the first time that such a circumstance has happened; though at different times different individuals have done it as they pafsed. – They repeated it two or three times; I was forced to bow to them, and immediately retired from the window.

Monday July 21. 1794

Mʳ Cline visited me. Pearson, the Warder a second time.

A most unpleasant story about Mʳ Frost and his behaviour to my maid – It has much distrefsed my family. The maid is gone, and a stranger come in her place. Mʳ Frost has very properly been refused admittance to my House.[94] – The villains who have taken me from my family without the slightest pretence! If there was not a Hell, it would be an impeachment of Providence.

Received my weekly pension £0. 13. 4

I have this day been <u>nine</u> weeks in CLOSE custody in the Tower. and hitherto without a pofsibility of forming the most distant conjecture concerning any charge to be brought against me.

TUESDAY July 22. 1794

The papers tell us, we are to be tried at the Old Bailey in September.

Wednesday. July 23. 1794

M.ʳ Cline visited me.

N.B. <u>Kinghorn</u>, the Gaoler, usually when he brings him up, desires M.ʳ Cline <u>not to stay long</u>.!!!

Thursday. July 24. 1794.

I have worked hard with my Chaucer.

There are 40 Warders; but only 20 attend, the other 20 have leave of absence. Ten have the care of the gate

p. 131 [*Top left-hand side. Here JHT made some jottings concerning the hierarchy of the Tower indicating something of his confusion in this regard.*]

Constable – Marquis Cornwallis

Governour – Gen.ˡ Vernon

Lieut. Governour

Deputy Lieutenant Governour. Col. Yorke

Fort Major

Yeoman Porter. L.ᵈ Cornwallis nephew, at school.[95]

Deputy Porter – Groz

132/33/r

and v   [*No diary entries.*]

134/35/r   FRIDAY. July. 25. 1794

I have this day, been <u>Ten</u> weeks in <u>CLOSE</u> custody.

In this so close custody I have had time to review my life that is pafsed; and I cannot find any one Action that I have committed, any word that I have written, any syllable that I have uttered, or any single thought that I have entertained, of a political nature, which I wish either to conceal or to recall.[96]

Saturday. July 26. 1794

Kinghorn tells me, that Joyce has permifsion to walk about the Tower. Kinghorn repeats to me <u>again</u> that he has orders to <u>sit close to me </u>and to <u>hear every word I speak to my surgeon</u>.

M.ʳ Cline visited me. Kinghorn close whilst operation.

Sunday July 27. 1794

Monday July 28. 1794
<Mould>↑<Jacks>↓ the Warder to attend me
I have this day, been TEN weeks in CLOSE custody in the
TOWER. I received £0. 13. 4.
Kinghorn says that a M! Trotter, son of D! Trotter[97] asked
affectionately after me, and said, he <u>was</u> a subscriber to my
Επεα Πτεροεντα.[98]
M! Cline visited me. Pafsed a Bougie, Kinghorn sitting by
all the while, saying he was so ordered to do, and did not
dare to do otherwise. Wallace told me this day, that
Governour Vernon, when he appointed him to afsist
Kinghorn, told Wallace, he was to stand close and listen to
every word; and that if any visitor, wife, child, or other,
spoke low, or spoke seditiously, or any thing improper,
Wallace should take them away and turn them out. So that
Gaolers and Warders are made Judges of sedition.
Miserable England!!
   M! Cline bro! me £20. 0. 0

134/35/v   I have in my pocket — £47. 13. 6
but I owe to M! Mould and to Nicholson about 3.13.6
          TUESDAY. July 29. 1794
yesterday M! Kyd sent the following letter to Privy Council
"My Lords
   "I presume there are only two objects which your lordships can have in view in my confinement: to prevent some
inconvenience, which it may pofsibly be supposed, would
arise to the public tranquility from my being at large; and
to secure my appearance to such prosecution as your lordships may think proper to institute against me. I am not
vain enough to suppose that the first ever entered much
into your lordships' consideration: neither my personal
importance nor my situation in life entitle me to that distinction. Taking it for granted therefore, that the only
object must be to secure my appearance to a prosecution, I
beg leave to observe, that that must be either for High-
treason, or for an inferior offence which <u>is bailable, in its
nature</u>. Should your lordships have determined on the first,
I can have nothing to request, but that it may be instituted

at an early period; but should your intentions be confined to the latter, I presume to make this further request, that I may be admitted to Bail. I might justly be accused of affectation, were I to pretend that, on the present occasion, liberty would not be more agreable to myself personally, than restraint; but I have relatives, some of whom reside at a great distance, whose feelings I wish to consult still more than my own. Should your lordships be disposed to admit me to Bail, I have persons to offer, to whose responsibility, I believe, no objection will be made. I have the honour to be,

My Lords,

etc.

p. 136
136/37/r

[*More financial jottings.*]

Wednesday July 30. 1794

A M.͏ʳ Crawford seized, and said to be a member of one of the suspected Societies, in all the papers – discharged, as soon as D. of Portland <u>came to town</u> !!!⁹⁹

THURSDAY. July 31. 1794

Cline visited, pafsed Bougie, Kinghorn sitting by.

	Paid				
By M.͏ʳ Cline	Blunt in full	8.	5.	0	
	Leaf in full	0.	10.	6	
	Treyer in full	· 3.	15.		
	Flight in full	2.	12.	<4>	
		15.	2.	6	

FRIDAY. AUGUST. 1. 1794

Kinghorn shews me an Order of Council dated July 30. 1794. giving <u>permifsion</u> to Governor or Deputy Governor, <u>to permit</u> at his <u>discretion</u> the Prisoners, to walk on Parade or Ramparts, or <u>where</u> he may think proper and at <u>what times</u> he may <u>judge fit</u>.

I have, this day been <u>**ELEVEN**</u> weeks in <u>**CLOSE**</u> custody; at this hot season and <u>uncommonly</u> hot summer in one room day and night, the same room, ↑for all occasions, natural, etc.↓ without a pofsibility of conjecturing charge.

It rained & blew. I walked out from ½ past five till 7.

SATURDAY August 2. 1794

M.͏ʳ Cline visited me. I met ↑M.͏ʳ Cline↓ at foot of staircase standing in pafsage, waiting for Kinghorn or Wallace.

It was forbidden by the <u>Governour</u>, that any visitor should walk with a prisoner. We retired to my room in about a quarter of an hour.

Rainy and windy day.

I walked from 8 in Evening till nine.

136/37/v   <center>SUNDAY August 3. 1794</center>

I applied through Kinghorn to the Governour, that Mould, my landlord, might continue to attend me, giving my reasons of more cleanlinefs and comfort. Kinghorn tells me, the Governour had no objection, but would send for Warders, and ask their choice, as he would give <u>them</u> no subject to complain. for they get about 14 shillings a week at gate and are allowed 17 shillings for attending prisoner. Warders, on application to them, chose to attend me by rotation weekly. ↑They always dine with me.↓ – The Governour <u>therefore</u> directed <u>their choice</u> to govern.

I am much <u>obliged</u> to the Governour, who promised me every indulgence in his power, when first I entered the Tower! Who seems to have an excellent notion of the dignity of his office! and a nice consideration of what is due to a Prisoner in his custody! – I have never seen him, except the first morning of my imprisonment. – "It is a gentle Jailor." and, a <u>wise</u> one, and has the feelings of a <u>gentleman</u>! and a high sense of honour.!!

I did wrong to apply to the governour, I should have <u>canvafsed</u> the Warders.

Monday August 4. 1794

Received – £0. 13. 4 . Jackson – the Warder. I had the first half pound of Snuff since payment of my bill by M<u>r</u> Cline.

I asked Kinghorn if I was permitted to go to the Record Office.[100] He would ask the governour. He came afterwards to tell me that no person was ↑at any time↓ permitted to see it without an order from Secretary of State; that the <u>Govern</u>our h<u>ad not</u> yet <u>seen</u> it.

p. 137 [*Top margin.*] Serj<u>t</u>. Adair[101] is retained – "King versus Horne Tooke." for High-treason: But what is the treason alleged, I cannot even conjecture.

[*Right margin.*] Aug<u>st</u>. 4. The first ½ Snuff

p. 138 [*Top margin.*] A Vest, silk from Fell and 1 pair breeches.

138/39/r   Tuesday August 5. 1794

Kinghorn tells me the Governour will see me in a few days.
D.ʳ Pearson visited me. brought me Zoo < >↑>nom<↓ia. by
D.ʳ Darwen.¹⁰² D.ʳ Pearson tells me that D.ʳ De Salis¹⁰³
exprefsed "his astonishment at the supposition that I was an
enemy to King & Lords; for that he (D.ʳ De Salis) was
present at the Crown and Anchor,¹⁰⁴ when they hooted and
hifsed me, for defending the Constitution and government
of England, by King, Lords and Commons." — This was
when <u>Newman</u> was Sheriff, who threatened me, upon
<u>Sheridan</u>'s motion: to which I wished an amendment lest
Sheridan's too general approbation of French revolution
should mislead men — "Not obtaining amendment, I made
a <u>separate subsequent motion and carried it.</u>" <u>Quod Vide</u>.¹⁰⁵
D.ʳ Pearson tells me, Major Cartwright¹⁰⁶ has been refused by
Privy Council to visit me. And that M.ʳ Bosville had applied
to M.ʳ Fawkener for permifsion to see me, and had been
refused by him, unlefs M.ʳ Bosville would declare upon his
honour, that he had some serious businefs with me.¹⁰⁷

                           Wednesday August 6. 1794

The report now is for a Special Commifsion on the 25.ᵗʰ of
August¹⁰⁸
M.ʳ Cline visited me.

> I paid M.ʳˢ Mould
> to this day
> 2.16. 6½

                           Thursday August 7. 1794
138/39/v   Friday August 8. 1794
Paid Nicholson to Monday August 4. Exclusive.
                      SATURDAY. Aug.ˢᵗ 9. 1794
M.ʳ Cline pafsed a Bougie. Kinghorn sitting by all the time.
D.ʳ Pearson visited me in the morning. i.e. at one o'clock
P.M.
Paid for my Newspapers, this day inclusive.
Saw M.ʳ Chatfield on the walks¹⁰⁹
                      SUNDAY. August 10.
Saw M.ʳ Bonney Mifs Johnson¹¹⁰ M.ʳˢ Tomkins and M.ʳ
Tomkins¹¹¹ on the walks

Monday Augst 11.

Newman, the new warder, by exchange with Lockhead.

Received £0.13.4.

Chatfield walked near Lady's walk in Tower

Tuesday August 12. 1794

Mr Cline pafsed a Bougie.

M^r {?M^{rs}} Tuffin {?Duffin}[112] sent me biscuits & brandy cherrie.

Wednesday August 13. 1794

Saw Mrs Bonney &c on the Walk

Thursday Augst 14.

Bought 3 p^r cotton 2 pair silk stock^{gs} – ↑Paid↓ 2. 2. 0

Ordered from Blunt 6 pair ruffles.[113]

Ordered from Leaf 1 pair shoes.

Friday August 15.

Mr Wardell of Trump Street sent me a brace of curious birds.[114] – I sent them to Mr Tuffin. Mrs Kyd stood under my window – "How do you do, madam?" "Very indifferently, not well at all."

Mr Wallace stepped forwards: and said – "This must not be suffered." and sent her off the Leads.

p. 139 [*Top margin.*] Mrs Martin says – there are five Indictments prepared by Wood for High-treason, against H. Tooke – Martin and three others

And four Indictments for sedition. But upon what grounds she could not learn.

Kyd is informed that there is only <u>one</u> indictment for High treason; and that that is not before Adair.

[*Right margin.*] August 14. 1794 Second ½ of snuff

[*Bottom margin.*] I learn from Mr Kyd, that attempts have been made to suborn witnefses against me. And from the best authority (the persons themselves) I know the wicked means employed by Reeves and Dundas with persons examined before the Privy Council

I defy them and their falsehood.

p. 140   # [*Financial calculations.*]

140/41/r   I have this day, been thirteen weeks, (a quarter of a year,) a CLOSE prisoner, without any <u>Charge</u>, without any hint from others, or <u>Conjecture</u> of my own, what can be the fact which will be brought against me, or the falsehood which may be fabricated.

SATURDAY August 1<7> >6<.1794

\# [*Financial calculations.*]

Spent in Tower . . . 60. 0. 0 in a quarter of a year Besides Grocer, my Garden. &c. Wright,
My imprisonment in the Tower is certainly at the rate of £300 per annum.
\# [*More financial calculations.*]

140/41/v Col. Kelly, with his wife, walked on broad walk in company with M.ʳ Stiles (Commiſs.ʳ of Customs) and his family, with M.ʳ Weston and his wife, and other ladies & gentlemen.[115] I took Weston by the hand; availing myself of the order, which only forbids <u>talking</u>.

D.ʳ Darwen in his <u>Zoonomia</u>[116]   ⎫   Bold men, to
D.ʳ Vincent in his <u>Greek Verb</u>[117] ⎬   praise me, at
D.ʳ Bedoes[118]   ⎭   this time.

SUNDAY August 1<8> >7< 1794

I have been now 13 weeks <u>Close</u> in the Tower.

MONDAY Aug.ˢᵗ 18

Cooper. the new Warder attended me.
Received – £0. 13. 4.
D.ʳ Pearson visited me. Read me a <u>part</u> of his Paper for transactions of Royal Society.[119] which he corrected with me.
M.ʳ Cline visited me & paſsed a bougie.

Tuesday August 19. 1794

Indictments for High treason in Scotland.[120]
Militia ↑Bill↓ discontent in London[121]

Wednesday August 20. 1794

Troops sent out of Tower – 100. Crimp's house in Shoe lane.[122] &c &c. &c.

Thursday August 2<0>>1<.1794

D.ʳ Pearson visited me, & finished reading his diſsertation for Royal society's transactions.
He told me some months ago, that a gentleman at Kensington brought him a paper relative to my complaint, which that gentleman received from one who felt very much for my situation, but he would not tell D.ʳ Pearson the name of the sender: This day D.ʳ Pearson tells me

142/43/r   that the person who sent these profefsions of respect and affection, with the paper, was M.ʳ Wilkes.¹²³

———————

About three hundred men in four Piquets marched at different times of the day out of the Tower to patrole the streets. – Not lefs than nine large concourses of People in nine different parts of the town this day, on the <u>Crimp</u> account as I learn from D.ʳ Pearson and M.ʳˢ Mould's sister, who saw them. – ½ past ten at night; I am told by Mould, the warder, that the people have thrown bricks, tiles, and jugs from top of houses, on the London horse afsociation,¹²⁴ and on the soldiers. And another Piquet is now marching from the tower.

p. 142 [*Top margin.*]

Since I am in the Tower
Dundas's Son
      and Nephew
and Rose's Son
Charles Dundas for Berkshire.
}
      members of Parl.ᵗ
      Represent the people.

[*Left margin.*]
The Alien Bill and Treyer naturalized.¹²⁵

142/43/r   FRIDAY. August 22 1794
(continued) M.ʳ Cline visited me, & pafsed a bougie. M.ʳˢ Tuffin sent me
      <2> >1< dozen of fine madeira and 1 doz. old Hock.
                 SATURDAY Aug.ᵗ 23
Kinghorn and Wallace come to me and tell me that the Colonel (who is just gone, I think they said Col. Frazer) and Adjutant Brice, had complained to the Governour, that the prisoners sat and talked together: that therefore the Governour ordered, that the prisoners should retire from the walks at sunset, and should not be permitted to speak to each other. – I refused to receive any orders but from the governor either by his own words spoken for himself, or written. and I desired Kinghorn to give my compliments to the Governour, and to tell him I desired to speak to him; having now been a quarter of a year and a week a CLOSE prisoner, and not having seen the Governour since the first day.

142/43/v SUNDAY August 24. 1794

At 11 o'clock the Dep.ʸ Lieut. Governour ↑{?Col} Yorke↓ visited me. He repeated his kind exprefsions and I believe his wishes to behave honourably are sincere. I made every apology for giving him the trouble to visit me. But I had now been in <u>CLOSE</u> custody 14 weeks in the tower, and had not seen him since the first day. that his handsome wishes were of little effect to us, if he left the prisoners at the mercy of every warder and every sentinel to harrafs and vex and degrade us. that I desired to receive his written orders for the daily changes which were made, not by him, but capriciously and insultingly by the underlings. That I had never spoken to a prisoner or to any person.[126] that I pafsed Col. Kelly on the walks and bowed. I pafsed Mʳ. Weston (in company with his wife & his father in law, Commifsioner Styles) and bowed. that when I met a Warder I asked after the health of his prisoner; that I had in silence given a pinch of snuff to a prisoner. If he had read the act of parlᵗ. by force of which we were detained, he would see that the Act only empowered <u>SAFE</u> custody; and we were kept in CLOSER custody than was used in the Bastile. that the order of the Privy Council that the prisoners should not talk together, could not mean to forbid, saying – "How do you do &c." that to retire at Sun set, in the heat of summer would deprive us of the benefit of the order of Privy Council. – That the order of the Warders attendance, had been referred to good pleasure of the <u>Warders</u>, without least regard to the prisoners. that I wished the Governour, after reading my letters not to send them <u>open</u> for whole garrison to peruse, but begged he would put a wafer. that Mʳ. Kinghorn thought himself bound to set by whilst Mʳ. Cline pafsed bougie. That Physician and surgeon often wait an hour and an hour and a half for admittance

144/45/r to me. I mentioned a cause of domestic uneasinefs, which made me wish to see two young ladies in my family: I asked him to attend them, instead of the Jailer; it being a delicate matter, and cruel to expose me to speak before Jailer and Warder.

The Governour ordered retreat at Sunset.

Said he would prevent Kinghorn sitting by at pafsing

bougie. – admitted that indifferent words might pafs between prisoners in presence and within hearing of Warders. That it was not Brice nor Frazer, but a <u>young</u> officer who gave information – that he would in future wafer my letters. – That Grauz, was director of Warders and followed antient rules. that he would attend my family any day at eleven o'clock – that he would tomorrow mention to Privy Council, that if they chose it I would change my surgeon and physician. – that he did ↑not↓ wish to aggravate our confinement, but feared Warders, might complain of him to L.ᵈ Cornwallis, Lieut. Governour. &c. That Grauz had been long time an Officer &c. (N. B. Grauz is a frenchman or Swifs, was servant to Earl Shipbrook, brother of Gen.ˡ Vernon; and has done duty only 4 years; and has of his own authority afsumed to give orders, and afterwards imposed on the Deputy Lieut. to give his sanction)

144/45/v

Monday Aug.ˢᵗ 25. 1794

Newman the Warder, by exchange with Hemings

New Order. M.ʳ Wallace alone is to carry newspapers!!! 9 times 9 – trots at least in a day.

M.ʳ Gruaz chuses to read them!!!

M.ʳ Cline pafsed a bougie.

Received – £0. 13. 4

An <u>order stuck up</u> in my room signed L. <u>Gruaz</u> ↑yeoman Porter.↓

TUESDAY. August 26. 1794

M.ʳ Kinghorn informs me that henceforward neither himself nor M.ʳ Wallace are to be present when my physician or surgeon is with me.

I sent no Newspaper this day to the prisoners.

Wednesday Aug.ˢᵗ 27. 1794.

M.ʳ Perry of Oxford Street, sent me a Pye.

Thursday. Aug.ˢᵗ 28 1794

M.ʳ Cline visited me, and pafsed a bougie, unattended (for the first time) by the Jailer.

Received ballance of   4. 17. 6. from M.ʳ Cline.

<Friday>↑> who paid me<↓ 15. 2. 6.

20. 0. 0

Friday August 29. 1794

#[*Some jotted accounts.*]
SATURDAY. August 30.

M[r.] Cline pafsed a bougie

By Governour's permifsion M[r.] Cline visited M[r.] Hardy whose wife died on thursday morning last.[127]

p. 145 [*Right margin.*] August 28 third ½ pound of Snuff
£0. 10. 6 due to Treyer

146/47/r
and v [*No diary entries.*]

p. 148 [*Top margin. JHT was an inveterate card player as the following jotting affirms:*]

Had 1 doz. Port from Wright Soho square		1. 2. 0
I owed to him before Cards	0. 15. 0	0. 18. 6
and once supper about	3. 6	2. 0. 6
	0. 18. 6	

[*Left margin.*] Saturday Sept[r.] 6. 1794 first ½ pound of snuff; but and one ½ for August 4. which I regret omitted to charge.

148/49/r
SUNDAY. August 31. 1794
Monday September 1. 1794

Paid to M[rs.] Mould, for August. 1794.	£2. 12. 11
Paid to Nicholson 4 Aug[st.] 31.inclusive.	1. 0. 10
Paid Treyer for snuff & Tobacco	0. 13. 0
Paid News to Sep[r.] 1.exclusive	1. 0. 3
Received £0. 13. 4	

Perry the Warder came.
Tuesday Sept[r.] 2. 1794

M[r.] Wallace spoke for damaged cannon to his nephew who deals with M[r.] Mangles, a ship carpenter.[128]
M[r.] Cline pafsed a bougie

Wednesday Sept[r.] 3. 1794

D[r.] Pearson showed me his syllabus of Lectures.

Thursday Sept[r.] 4. 1794

M[r.] Cline gave me a brace of partridges which I gave to Kinghorn.

Friday. Sept[r.] 5.1794

Saturday. Sept.̇ 6. 1794.

M.̇ Bonney, feverish. At 7 this morning I sent a note to Doctor Pearson, begging to see him.

M.̇ Cline visited me.

D.̇ Vincent. M.̇ John Pearson.[129]

Sunday. Sept.̇ 7. 1794

Violent cold. Head-ache. &c.

Monday Sept.̇ 8. 1794

D.̇ Pearson

Received   £0. 13. 4.

148/49/v   Tuesday Sept.̇ 9. 1794

£20. 11. 0

Wednesday Sept.̇ 10. 1794

"Begs M.̇ Cline[130] to thank M.̇ and M.ṛ Macnamara for their kind visit to his girls. M.̇ H. T. has no doubt of their friendship, though he has not been a friendly correspondent to them. M.̇ H. T. has however corresponded with M.̇ Macnamara more than with any other person: for he wrote to him <u>twice</u> in <u>four</u> years. He has not done so much to <u>any one else</u>. An odd circumstance, for a man to say this, who is in <u>close</u> custody for High-treason.

M.̇ H. T. remembers with pleasure the many happy hours he has past with M.̇ and M.ṛ Macnamara: and doubts not that he shall still spend with them many more as happy. He longs to see all their family: and shall be very proud, if his young friend John remembers him. But he regrets that he will not any longer be the same little John that he used to kifs till his father was jealous. However M.̇ H. T. declares that he will shake him by the hand in spite of M.̇ Macnamara.

M.̇ Macnamara will wonder perhaps to be told, that M.̇ H. T. lived two years at Wimbledon, with a nice horse in his stable, and the use of his own Legs; and yet never rode out once, nor ever took a walk on the outside of his own gates. He went to town in a chaise about thirty times in a year, always to dine in company. On the sundays, during winter and spring, he had usually from 12 to 20 persons, to eat (literally Mutton) with him at Wimbledon. The rest of his time was devoted to hard labour in his garden (which has driven off the Gout) and to his books, with a game at

150/51/r   cards every evening with his girls, who have been constantly imprisoned at Wimbledon with him.

M.ʳ Macnamara's <u>Chests</u>, <u>harpsichord</u>, <u>table</u> and <u>Casks</u> are all in perfect safety; and M.ʳ H. T. thinks himself as safe as any of them, though not so pleasantly situated. M.ʳ H. T. has always been from his cradle as great a Traitor as he is at this moment; and shall certainly continue the same to the end of his life: concerning the period of which, whether long or short, he is neither more nor lefs solicitous than he has always been. It has been a very happy one; it is now happy: and has never been, and he trusts it never will be, embittered by the fear of losing it.

He writes quick. He can write but little. He will talk the more when he meets his old friends.

M.ʳ H. T. is very anxious to be told that M.ʳˢ Macnamara is in perfect health and happinefs.

Thirty years ago M.ʳ H. T. has seen the Bastille, and known many persons who had been imprisoned there: Their treatment was much better, and much lefs degrading than that which the prisoners experience in the Tower. M.ʳ H. T. has however lefs reason to complain than any one there: and in respect to his books and papers, the Privy Council behaved well: for they took care that they should not be mislaid or deranged or stolen or lost. They did well: for H. T. could not have gone over the same labour again: and they contain immense preparations, which none ever yet made, for information important to the rest of the world, as well as to England and the present day; which no man is likely to give but himself.[131]

150/51/v   M.ʳ Macnamara's friendship for M.ʳ H. T. need not give M.ʳ Macnamara any uneasinefs: for H. T. has never done an action, nor uttered a word, nor written a single sentence, nor harboured a thought, of an important political nature, which (taken with all its circumstances of time, place, and occasion) he wishes either recalled or concealed."

———

For thee, fair freedom, welcome all the past:
For thee, fair freedom, welcome even the last.[132]

———

Thursday Sept.ʳ 11. 1794.

Mʳ Cline pafsed a bougie.

I received from him	10.	10.	0
He gave to my family last week	6.	6.	0
	16.	16.	0

#[*Financial calculations.*]

p. 151   #[*Financial calculations.*]

p. 152   #[*Financial calculations.*]

152/53/r   Friday Sept.ʳ 12. 1794

All the Papers announce a Special Commifsion.

Seventeen weeks in Custody.

Saturday. Sept.ʳ 13. 1794

The Deputy Lieut. Governor is gone (they say) for a Week.

Gruaz insulted Mʳ Thelwall.

Gruaz told him, he was an impertinent fellow. The <u>Major</u> of the Tower[133] followed – <u>took Thelwall by the arm</u>, and ordered the Warder at his peril to take care that – "<u>that man</u> should not walk tomorrow, but from ten to four or five."

Sunday Sept.ʳ 14. 1794

The Major of Tower ordered the Retreat to be beat at ¼ before six – instead of 20 min. after six.

The Major has given the Centinels strict charge of the prisoners, telling them that the Warders do not perform their duty. &c. &c.

Monday. Sept.ʳ 15. 1794

Seventeen weeks in the Tower.

Received £0. 13. 4

Paid Mʳˢ Mould to Sept.ʳ 14. inclusive 2. 4. 9½

    Nicholson

Dawson, the Warder came

Mʳ Cline pafsed bougie.

The Major sent a Serj.ᵗ to Cap.ᵗ Dalling[134] for talking to me.

152/53/v   Tuesday Sept.ʳ 16. 1794

#[*Financial jottings.*]

Wednesday Sept.ʳ 17.

    Intelligence of a Special Commifsion, with a variety of particular circumstances, all satisfying me, that there is a deep conspiracy for deliberate murder; and for putting the lash hand[135] to the old Laws and constitution.

I do not wish to survive them.

———

Dᵣ Pearson visited me
                    Thursday Septᵣ 18. 1794
Mᵣ Cline paſsed bougie
                    Friday Septᵣ 19.
                    Saturday. Septᵣ 20. 1794.
Mᵣ Cline paſsed bougie. Gave me   £10. 0. 0
    Mᵣ Cline Septᵣ 11   10. 10. 0
      Mᵣ Cline to my family about 5 Septᵣ   6. 6. 0
Quære what has Mᵣ Cline given to my   26. 16. 0
family since ? ? ?
Septᵣ 18 Mᵣ Cline to Wildman for Hart   10. 0. 0
                                             36. 16. 0

Paid newspapers this Evening in full
Wright sent a dozen of Port, a 2ᵈ time
and had a dozen of empty bottles
I owe to him   2 dozen Port
                                      1 dozen of bottles

p. 153 [*Right margin.*] Treyer Septᵣ 18
                                s.   d.
2ᵈ ½ pound snuff due – 10.   6
Wright due to him 2 dry Port
                1 doz. bottles.

p. 154 [*Top margin.*]
Received cash –   100. 12. 6
Septᵣ 20. Cline. Dᵒ   10. 0. 0
                        110. 12. 6

154/55/r   Sunday Septᵣ 21. 1794
                (In my Drawer: a Reserve of £20)
    In pocket   14. 16. 8
    I owe to Nicholson to this day ⎱   1. 1. 0
    inclusive   ⎰ 1. 0. 8
    To Mʳˢ Mould only from
    Septᵣ 14 – – ? – –
    ↑I owe↓ nothing for Newspaper, Barber, or anything else

I shall receive tomorrow   0. 13. 4
                                                            16. 11. 0

Agreed that M.ʳ Joyce's brother shall employ Gurney &
Ramsey[136] to take down Judge's charge for Joyce Bonney
Kyd and H Tooke – and that four copies shall be immediately delivered, one to each of the above. at our joint
expence.

Monday. Sept.ʳ 22. 1794

Blower. Warder

Received   0. 13. 4
More wisdom in Capt. Morris's Song in this day's Morning
Chronicle than is to be found in most volumes.[137]

Tuesday Sept.ʳ 23. 1794

#[*More accounts.*]
M.ʳ Cline paſsed a bougie.
Felix Vaughan is not come <u>yet</u> to town!
M.ʳ Cline launced my gum

154/55/v

Wednesday Sept.ʳ 24. 1794

Thursday Sept.ʳ 25. 1794

½ pound of snuff the third, besides Aug.ˢᵗ 4

                                   had   15. 6. 0
at night – – – 14. 12. 0   have   14. 12. 0
                                             0. 14. 0 spent

FRIDAY Sept.ʳ 26. 1794

In Special commiſsion ⎧   Grose . <u>Lawrence</u>
11 Counsel   ⎪   <u>Eyre</u>   <u>Buller</u>
                       ⎪   <u>Macdonald</u> . Hotham
They evidently   ⎪   Recorder <u>Rose</u>. Com. Serj.ᵗ Syl<u>ves</u>ter
mean a decided,   ⎬   Serj.ᵗ <u>Rigby</u>
long-prepared   ⎪   Main<u>w</u>aring
  Murder   ⎪   S.ʳ <u>Charles</u> Morgan
                       ⎪   Joddrell
SOIT   ⎩   <u>Wegg</u> &c.[138]

M.ʳ Perry[139] sent me Turtle Suop

––––––––

Tom Symonds tells me M.ʳ Joyce's brother that a friend of
his, who dined with M.ʳ Pitt the day before yesterday, in
company with Attorney Gen.ˡˢ &c. &c. told Symonds, he

heard M.ʳ Pitt say, that they had not been able to get any thing against M.ʳ Horne Tooke.[140]

M.ʳ Cline paſsed a bougie.

I have this day been 19 weeks in <u>close</u> custody

p. 155 [*Right margin.*] Sept.ʳ 25 1794 3.ᵈ ½. Snuff due 0. 14. 0

156/57/r
and v   [*No diary entries.*]
158/59/r   Saturday Sept.ʳ 27. 1794
M.ʳ Cline – to call on W. Tooke who called on me (coming from Brighton) before he went home
                  Sunday Sept.ʳ 28
M.ʳ Cline with M.ʳ Tooke's affectionate meſsage. – My answer
                  Monday Sept.ʳ 29
                                    Bateman Warder
Just two ↑or three↓ days before Grand Jury, Rumour in papers of a Plot to aſsaſsinate the King. – The villains have <u>timed</u> this well, to destroy whom they please.[141]
     Received   0. 13. 4
Due only to M.ʳˢ Mould   13. 16. 10.
from Sept.ʳ 14 exclusive
M.ʳ Cline paſsed a bougie. M.ʳ Tooke's heart smites him at last. I shall be able to pay my attorney to subpœna my witneſses.
          I understand that two most execrable schemes of the Ministry for our destruction are detected and will be exposed.[142]
My Warder, Bateman is a shocking Beast, loaded with nauseous infirmities, and a most brutal mind and manners. To be stapled to the floor, without him, would be more tolerable than his company.
158/59/v   Tuesday Sept.ʳ 30. 1794
D.ʳ Pearson visited me.   <13. 11. 0>
M.ʳ Cline visited me.
Wright sent me a doz. Port. a 3.ᵈ time.
I had 1 doz bottles.
                  Wednesday.<Sept.ʳ 30.>↑>October.1.<↓ 1794

Paid Mould – 1. 18. 5½   £13. 11. 0
                                          1. 18. 5½
                  {?Restent}   11. 12. 6½

F—— wished to speak to me, and was prevented by Bateman, the Warder[143]

Thursday October 2.

Privy Council deny Clarkson[144] permifsion to see me, telling him – "it would be time enough when the bills are found"

N. B. The Commifsioners go from Serjeant's Inn at ¼ past 9 this morning.

M.ʳ Cline gave me   - -   28. 0. 0

See Sept.ʳ 20. ↑or 17.ᵗʰ↓ to my family   70.

#[*Financial jottings.*]

Oct.ʳ 2. Grand Jury commence

p. 159   #[*Tally of weeks in the Tower and port/wine account details.*]
160/61/r   #[*Financial jottings.*]

Friday Oct.ʳ 3. 1794

M.ʳ Cline pafsed a bougie.

Gave to a corporal for his humanity to his recruits £1. 1. 0 which I sent the Warder M.ʳ Warner. a {?honorarium}

Saturday Oct.ʳ 4.

#[*Financial jottings.*]

M.ʳ Cline visited me and brought me a pair of buckles

I have likewise from him Wyvill's 3. Vol.ˢ [145]

M.ʳˢ Piozzi's   2 Vol[146]

Col. Money's book[147]

Bandages

King's speeches[148]

Copy of Morning Post and Chronicle 14.ᵗʰ July 1790[149]

Reports of Lords &/ Commons.[150]

160/61/v   Sunday October. 5. 1794

Grand Jury have not yet found any bill.[151]

Joyce gave me a copy of Eyre's Charge,[152] taken by Ramsey.

Capt. Chivers called to speak to me in the Tower — grateful young man.[153]

————

M.ʳ Campbell, of Grand Jury produced a Letter to the Court[154]

Monday Oct.ʳ 6.
M.ʳ Cline pafsed a bougie
Mould, new Warder.

162/63/r   Tuesday October 7. 1794
My Lord Chief Justice
I have received this afternoon from M.ʳ White Solicitor of
the Treasury, and Solicitor for the prosecution, the under-
mentioned notice[155]

———

"John Horne Tooke, Clerk
&c
My Lord, this notice is perfectly nugatory to me: for I am
in such <u>Close</u> custody, that I have no means of availing
myself of this notice: as I am not permitted to see any person whatever, except my surgeon and physician; who, if
either of them should happen to call upon me, are not persons to employ in such a businefs.

I apprehend besides, my Lord, that the Solicitor of
the Treasury, has, by his own authority, narrowed even the
miserable means which the narrowest interpretation of the
Law allows me for my defence. I suppose that my Solicitor
is not to be afsigned by the Court. Neither do I understand
what M.ʳ White means by – "such accefs as shall be <u>just and
reasonable</u>".

My Lord, I have no books to consult; but, I
believe, I am entitled to chuse my own solicitor, without
afsignment. and, I believe, I am by Law entitled, not only
to my Counsel and Solicitor, but also to such agents as I
shall find necefsary for my defence. and that they may have
162/63/v   accefs to me at all – <u>seasonable hours.</u>
My Lord, I understand, and the Law will understand, what
<u>seasonable</u> hours mean, but not what <u>just and seasonable</u>
accefs means.

p. 164   #[*Snuff account.*]

164/65/r   Tuesday Oct.ʳ 7. 1794
½ pound snuff by M.ʳ Warner.
notice of Bill found[156]
Clarkson called – I gave him list of my witnefses
to subpœna.

Wednesday Octr. 8. 1794

My nephew John Wildman,   #[*Financial jottings.*]
came to me this day, by
permifsion of Privy Council.
Clarkson, my solicitor, applied
for him last friday, to afsist
my preparation by writing
for me.

Thursday Octr. 9

Erskine, Gibbs, Vaughan & Clarkson visited me. I see that
I must plead for myself in person.[157]
Mr Cline saw me in the Evening.

I learn from Vaughan, that Mr Tooke deposited with him
for me £100 and that Mr Cline, on Vaughan's note,
advanced to him for me, also £100.

164/65/v   [*No diary entries.*]
166/67/r   Friday October. 10. 1794.
Goose to Kyd and Bonney
Saturday Octr. 11.

D^r. Pearson called   #[*Financial jottings.*]
     I saw Perry pafs by.
  A note from Clarkson, my solicitor, that the Indictments
would be delivered on monday ↑the 13th ↓ and the Trials
commence on monday the 27th. of this month.
Mr Cline called in the Evening.
Sunday October. 12. 1794

Mr Cline called.
Clarkson had promise from Privy Council that my nephew
Wildman should have accefs to me.
Monday Oct. 13.   Cooper new Warder

White served me with copies of Indictment and Lists of
Witnefses 207 and Jurors 228.[158]

	207		
---	---	---	To inquire after
	228		43 and ½ per day
	435		besides my own witnefses
Out of 228 Jurors			to produce – and all other
I see 11 honest men.[159]			preparations.

166/67/v   Tuesday – Cline
                             Wednesday – Cline

For Martin to Clarkson for Dixon   £10. 10. 0
½ pound Snuff. Paid in full   £ 1. 1. 0
                Thursday Octr. 16. 1794
To Mefs^{rs}. Clarkson –   £200
                Friday Octr. 17. 1794
M^r. Cline
                Saturday Octr. 18. 1794
M^r. Cline
                Sunday Octr. 19
M^r. Cline
                Monday Octr. 20
Newman, new Warder
Received – £0. 13. 4
Cline came.
                Tuesday. Octr. 21
                Wednesday Octr. 22[160]
I saw Rich^d. Sharpe.[161]
M^r. Cline came
                Thursday Octr. 23. 1794
I paid M^{rs}. Mould £4. 19. 2½ in full
Erskine and Gibbs are to dine with me and settle and
arrange for my trial <u>tomorrow</u>. They are to come at ½ past
3 M^r. Cline came, and at Nine at night whilst M^r. Cline and
my nephew were

p. 167   #[*Snuff account.*]
168/69/r
and v   [*No diary entries.*]
170/71/r
and v   [*No diary entries.*]
172/73/r
and v   [*No diary entries.*]
174/75/r   with me. Kinghorn the Jailer, came to lock me up, as usual,
M^r. Cline and my nephew were preparing to depart.
Kinghorn gave me the Governor's compliments and
informed me, that the Sheriff would take me tomorrow at
Eight in the morning to convey me to Newgate — Short
notice for a removal, especially with my infirmity.
— By this method, they embarrafs and harrafs us just at the
moment of preparing for trial, and interrupt our
businefs – This rancour is like all that has preceded.

Friday Octr. 24. 1794

I rose at four, because of my infirmity that I might be ready at eight for the sheriff.

I packed up my papers in a trunk; my things in a box lent to me by M^{rs}. Mould.

Half past six o'clock – Kinghorn tells me that I am to walk thro' the tower on foot and there to be delivered to the Sheriff. I desired my compliments to the Governor, and my thanks for all the civilities and indulgences – (small enough God knows) – which I have received in the Tower – at the same to {?reproach} to him, that it is wet above and below, 174/75/v that my gouty feet compel me to wear thin shoes, being unable to bend a strong sole or strong upper leather: that it would be cruel just at this moment to make me catch cold, and thus carry me a <u>dumb</u> man to my trial: that there is chance enough of that in the sudden change of my bed and apartments: – and therefore to request that I may go in a coach to the Gate of the tower; and if it is necefsary that I should be delivered on foot, that I may there descend, and be so delivered.

I expect Governor's answer,

He permitted a coach

We are paraded, with great attendance, slowly thro' <u>St. Paul's church yard</u> to Newgate[162]

Thus I lose my consultation with Erskine and Gibbs.[163]

Sheriff very civil.

Saturday Octr. 25.

Arraigned.

Received by Wildman, from Vaughan

£30

Sheriff very civil.

176/77/r
and v   [*No diary entries.*]
178/79/r
and v   [*No diary entries.*]
180/81/r   Tuesday Octr. 28.1794

M^r. Cline this evening put into my hand a Letter which he desired me to read when he was gone. It contained only 5. ten pound Bank notes – £50.

[*Horne Tooke's trial took place at the Old Bailey between 17 and 22 November 1794.*]

Sunday Nov.ʳ 23. Mʳ Cline put into my hand £30
Wimbledon. Arrived at 3 o'clock P. M.
Tuesday Novʳ 25 1794. Bank notes 100. 0. 0
Gold   3. 3. 0
Silver   0. 12. 0
_____
103. 15. 0

180/81/v   Tooke   100
Cline   100   from
Macnamara   100   Gawler
_____
300

[*Here, for our purposes, the diary ends. In the second volume of* DoP *there are a number of fragments of a political nature interspersed amongst JHT's editorial notes for the second edition of* The Diversions of Purley, *but they belong to a later date.*]

NOTES TO TEXT OF DIARY

[1] These were perhaps potential defence witnesses, or persons likely to be willing to stand surety for Horne Tooke if he was released on condition of good behaviour. See Biographical Index for the duke of Richmond and John Cartwright.

[2] The quotation is from Geoffrey Chaucer's translation of Boethius, *De Consolatione Philosophiae*. Rogers mentions that JHT had a copy of Chaucer's works in the Tower, and an editor's footnote remarks that it was an old 'black-letter copy which he afterwards gave to Mr Rogers'. The note also mentions that Horne Tooke, while in the Tower, made many notes in the margin of the first book of 'Boethius, de Consolatione Philosophiae' (G. H. Powell (ed.), *Reminiscences and Table-Talk of Samuel Rogers, Banker, Poet & Patron of the Arts 1763–1855*, collected from the original memoirs of Dyce and Sharpe, with introduction and index (London, 1903), p. 96).

[3] In making this list of names and events Horne Tooke is evidently sorting out his thoughts and perhaps his strategy for defence. Nearly all the names and events are identifiable within the context of Horne Tooke's political and personal activities from the mid-1760s. Like the rest of the diary up till 24 May they were written initially in pencil and subsequently gone over in ink.

[4] Horne Tooke knew several Pearsons. See 102/03/v for Sir Richard Pearson, n. 58 for Dr. George Pearson, and n. 129 for John Pearson. But the dinner, which was held at Spitalfields, was at the house of Michael Pearson, the apothecary (possibly the brother of Sir Richard Pearson), Horne Tooke's 'gentle and amiable friend . . . forty long years my steady and uniform accomplice and comforter in all my treasons' (*The Diversions of Purley Part II* (London, 1805), p. 193). Cf. J. Ann Hone, 'Radicalism in London, 1796–1802, convergences and continuities', in John Stephenson (ed.), *London in the Age of Reform* (Oxford, 1977), pp. 79–101, at p. 93. See Peter Barfoot and John Wilkes (compilers), *The Universal British Directory of Trade, Commerce and Manufacture . . .* (2nd edn., London, [1793]), p. 451 s.v. 'Apothecaries', for Michael Pearson's Spitalfields address. He was a member of the SCI.

[5] The letter mentioned (intercepted by the authorities) was from Jeremiah Joyce (see Biographical Index) to Horne Tooke, 12 May, in which Joyce, reporting to Horne Tooke the arrest of Hardy, used the phrase, 'Is it possible to get ready by Thursday?', referring to the preparation of a pamphlet listing the government sinecures of the Grenvilles (Pitt's cousins) taken from the Court Calendar, the aim of which was to discredit Pitt.

The connection with the Pearson dinner was that it was held on the particular Thursday that Joyce had mentioned in the letter, and on that day Horne Tooke and his dining companions noted the presence of the light horse on the streets nearby. From this Horne Tooke deduced that the authorities had supposed Joyce's words to refer to an insurrection and were taking appropriate precautions. At his trial he forced the prosecution to produce the letter and used it effectively in his own defence, suggesting that it had been the letter and the authorities' wholly mistaken interpretation of it that had led to his arrest. See T. B. and T. J. Howell (compilers), *A Complete Collection of State Trials and Proceedings for High Treason and Other Crimes and Misdemeanors*, 33 vols. (London, 1816–26), xxv (35 & 36 George III ... A.D. 1794–1796) (London, 1818), cols. 248–50. However, although Joyce was interrogated about it in the Privy Council (PRO PC 2/140 14 May), there is no other evidence that the prosecution intended to use the letter or that the authorities had, in fact, so interpreted it in the first place; at least not to the extent of arresting Horne Tooke solely on its account. It is unlikely that Joyce was arrested directly on account of it either, since his identification as secretary to the joint Committee of Secrecy (or Correspondence) of the SCI and LCS was known previously; it was this, as we shall see, which formed the basis of the crown's case against the twelve and which led to their being charged with high treason.

But these brief notes in Horne Tooke's prison diary do suggest that he did believe that the interception of the letter was fundamental, and that it had not simply been a clever court-room ploy on his part in order to convince the jury that his arrest had been the result of a ridiculous error by a jittery administration rather than of any long-held suspicion of him founded on his political activities. At the same time, it would be mistaken to believe that Horne Tooke was being totally ingenuous about the reasons for his arrest. As the most prominent member of the SCI still active in London, and with the SCI moving closer and closer towards the politically more extreme and proliferating LCS (see n. 9), he was arrested probably as a matter of course. He had been named by the LCS spy, John Taylor, incorrectly as it turned out, as an SCI delegate to the joint SCI/LCS committee as early as 22 April (Mary Thale (ed.), *Selections from the Papers of the London Corresponding Society 1792–1799* (Cambridge, 1983), p. 144). And, as his biographers pointed out, he was well aware before his arrest that government spies, one of whom was probably the member of parliament, John Wharton, were acting within his own social circle (Alexander Stephens, *Memoirs of J. Horne Tooke*, 2 vols. (London, 1813), II, p. 116; Minnie Clare Yarborough, *John Horne Tooke* (New York, 1926), p. 155). The *DNB* is probably wrong, however, to suggest, as it does, that Horne Tooke was playing at treason and that the Joyce letter was an elaborate game of political chicken.

[6] Evan Nepean, until July 1794 under-secretary of state for the Home Department. See Biographical Index.

[7] John Reeves, best known as the founding spirit of the contentious patriotic associations but without any recorded official position *vis-à-vis* the Privy Council. See Biographical Index for a discussion of his possible role.

[8] Henry Dundas, until July 1794 home secretary. See Biographical Index.

[9] The Society for Constitutional Information (SCI), founded by Major Cartwright and others in 1780, was the older and more patrician reform society, of which Horne Tooke was a leading member. The London

Corresponding Society (LCS), founded in January 1792 by the shoemaker, Thomas Hardy, had a mass membership of over 5,000 men; it was potentially much more dangerous in the eyes of the authorities than the SCI. At Horne Tooke's trial in 1794 the solicitor general reckoned membership at possibly 8,000 (T. B. and T. J. Howell (compilers), op. cit. (note 5), xxv (35 & 36 George III . . . A.D. 1794–1796) (London, 1818), col. 38). A figure of 10,000 is suggested by Cannon (John Cannon, *Parliamentary Reform, 1640–1832* (Cambridge, 1973), p. 135), while Brown presents evidence to suggest between 5,000 and 10,000 (Philip A. Brown, *The French Revolution in English History* (London, 1923), p. 59). But John Binns, at one time chairman, reckoned, on the basis of the society's accounts, that for several years the figures for membership were probably between 18,000 and 20,000 (John Binns, *Recollections of the Life of John Binns . . . written by himself* (Philadelphia, 1854), p. 46). JHT's biographer Alexander Stephens (op. cit. (note 5), vol. II, p. 82) assessed its membership at between 25,000 and 30,000.

Horne Tooke was never a member of the LCS, but his growing association with its leadership together with the move for actual amalgamation of the SCI with the LCS was at the root of the administration's distrust and fear of him. It was the LCS's defiant resolution at the mass meeting at Chalk Farm of 14 April 1794 to press on with the formation of a national convention in London, in spite of the suppression of the Scottish and British conventions in Edinburgh the previous year, and the subsequent decision to establish a Committee of Secrecy (or Correspondence) between the two societies, presumably for this purpose, which provoked the authorities into action.

Horne Tooke's involvement with the LCS had begun early: according to Stephens he assisted in drawing up the rules of the society after Hardy had approached him (op. cit. (note 5), vol. II, p. 82). After his acquittal Horne Tooke declared to the court that he had merely corrected the document and that he would correct any man's work, citing the case of his even having corrected a work of criticism against himself (*The Proceedings at Large on the Trial of John Horne Tooke for High Treason taken in short-hand by J. H. Blanchard*, 2 vols. (London, 1795), II, p. 466). But the links between Horne Tooke, the SCI, and the LCS were much closer than this (See J. Ann Hone, op. cit. (note 4), *passim*, but especially p. 83; Philip A. Brown, op. cit. (note 9), pp. 53, 58; and PRO TS 11/951/3493 and 3495).

[10] The Privy Council Register's account of Horne Tooke's examination by the Privy Council of 16 May (PRO PC 2/140) is unfortunately not verbatim, but something of the tone as well as the content of the interview can nevertheless be gauged. It began with Dundas's statement, recorded as follows:

That the nature of the Treasonable Practices for which he had been apprehended, and of which it was conceived he was guilty, were, that he had been a leading and active member of the Two Societies, . . . ; that the object of these Societies now evidently was to form a National Convention, in order to supersede the Established and legal Government of the Country, and it was to this point, that it was intended to Examine him, and with a view of giving him an opportunity of removing the suspicions entertained on that head.

This was the signal of course (as with other examinations) for the examinee to give evidence against anyone he could think of. But Horne Tooke's response was characteristically attacking rather than defensive and evidently not bereft of his celebrated wit:

Mr Horne Tooke asked if it could be imagined that it was sufficient to justify the holding him in custody, the taking possession of his House, and seizing his papers, that it was conceived he had been guilty of Treasonable practices. That if the Lord Chancellor or Mr Dundas, or any other Member of the Privy Council, would, upon their Honour, assure him that there had been any Information upon Oath against him for Practices full of Treason, for that he understood Treasonable Practices to mean, or any one Act of Treason, He would not ask who the Informant was, or what the particular Charge was, He would answer any Questions that might be put to him, and be Examined to the utmost extent Their Lordships pleased; — Upon being told that no such assurance would be given him, and that in the present stage of the Business it was not necessary that any such assurance should be given; but that he certainly was not obliged to answer at all. He said that in consequence of that refusal, he did refuse to be Examined.

He complained of the hardship of having been apprehended, and of having his Papers and Books and his Family at the Mercy of the Persons who had executed the Warrant against him, and were in his House; but he admitted they had behaved perfectly well, and said if he was a Traitor he had been used too well, but if not too ill —

He was then desired to withdraw.

Horne Tooke expanded on the details of his examination in a note in the margins of the copy of Chaucer's rendering of Boethius which he had with him in the Tower (see n. 2):

Mr Dundas, Secretary of State, told me in the Privy Council that 'It was *conceived* that I was guilty of treasonable practices.' He refused to tell me *by whom* it was conceived. I offered to be examined *to any extent*, if the Chancellor or Dundas would declare that there was *any* treason. The Chancellor said that I seemed to object to the legality of the *warrant*; but that I might object to that hereafter in another place.

Editor's note in G. H. Powell (ed.), op. cit. (note 2), p. 96, adds further information: 'Horne Tooke remarks that he afterwards learnt that at that very moment a bill was brought into the House of Commons to legalise the warrant, and to indemnify the Ministers for issuing it'. This was the Habeas Corpus Suspension Bill, for which see the following note.

[11] The Habeas Corpus Suspension Bill, 'An Act to impower his Majesty to secure and detain such Persons as his Majesty shall suspect of conspiring against his Person and Government', passed in the House of Commons in two divisions, 16 and 17 May 1794. It received the royal assent and became law on 23 May. Horne Tooke's point is that the bill was rushed through parliament in order to legalize the holding of prisoners without charge.

[12] Almost certainly a reference to James Walsh, identified as a spy by John Groves (himself a spy) at the Chalk Farm meeting of 14 April in order to pro-

tect his own cover ('The Trial of Thomas Hardy for High Treason', in T. B. and T. J. Howell (compilers), op. cit. (note 5), XXIV (34 & 35 George III . . . A.D. 1794) (London, 1818), cols. 758–60). John Richter in the manuscript account of his arrest and interrogation (British Library, Additional MS 27816 fo. 451ff., p. 14 of Richter account) states that Walsh, a spy, led the band of officers who arrested Thelwall; see also col. 554 of 'The Trial of Thomas Hardy for High Treason' for mention of Walsh being present at the arrest of Isaac Saint of the Norwich Constitutional Society. Walsh *père* was presumably the member of the SCI of that name. Walsh is mentioned in the records of the SCI generally and in 1792 as having given £2. 11*s*. 0*d*. towards the 'Subscription . . . for the purpose of assisting the efforts of France in the cause of Freedom' (PRO TS 11/951/3495).

[13] These were all held in the Tower on a charge of high treason. The names are written directly in ink and must have been added after 24 May, when he was allowed access to pen, ink, and paper for the first time.

John Richter, member of the SCI. See Biographical Index.

John Augustus Bonney, member of the SCI. See Biographical Index.

John Thelwall, member of the Southwark Friends of the People and of the LCS. See Biographical Index.

Revd. Jeremiah Joyce, member of the SCI. See n. 5 and Biographical Index.

John Lovett (Lovet/Loveit/Lovatt), member of the LCS. See Biographical Index.

The three following were incarcerated on different dates, which explains why they are listed in a separate column by Horne Tooke in the right-hand margin, presumably at a later date:

Thomas Hardy, secretary of the LCS. Although arrested on 12 May, he was held in the custody of the messenger, John Gurnell, and not incarcerated in the Tower till 29 May. See Biographical Index.

John Martin, member of the LCS and associate member of the SCI. See Biographical Index. He was in the King's Bench prison for debt at the time of the arrests (See pencil note to that effect beside his name on a list of those with warrants out against them (PRO TS 11/957/3502/1 fo. 60). John Bayley, using the Tower Committal Lists, says he was 'committed by order of the court of the King's Bench, in Easter term' (3–29 May) (John Bayley, *The History and Antiquities of the Tower of London,* . . . 2 parts (London, 1821, 1825), II, p. 621). Horne Tooke's entry for 31 May mentions Martin's arrival in the Tower.

Stuart (or Stewart) Kyd (or Kydd), member of the SCI. See Biographical Index. Committed to the Tower on 6 June. See, for Kyd's arrival, Horne Tooke's entry for 7 June. Up till 4 June Kyd had been permitted to remain at his own chambers because he was about to publish a work on corporations 'which was nearly finished' (PRO PC 2/140 fo. 263, printed pagination 129); presumably this was volume II of his *A Treatise on the Law of Corporations*, 2 vols. (London, 1793, 1794). The permission was a demonstration of courtesy quite remarkable considering the gravity of the charge against him. Like Sharp, however, he was under guard. At a subsequent examination by the Privy Council of 4 June he was to be permitted again to return to his own chambers but opted instead to be in custody at the messenger's house. It might be interpreted from this that he was suffering harassment from the guards assigned to him at his chambers, who in contrast to the messengers may have appeared less well bred. Holcroft, who visited Sharp at his house while so guarded, was harassed, and remarked on the difference in class between the guards and the messengers (Thomas Holcroft, *A Narrative of Facts, relating to a Prosecution for High Treason* (London, 1795), pp. 92–96).

It was not till Kyd's final examination of 6 June that he was committed to the Tower. The reason seems unclear — even arbitrary — and may have had more to do with his giving personal offence by his off-hand manner and refusal to provide information than with any treasonable act which the Privy Council actually believed him to have committed. He was, however, identified as having been a member of the joint LCS/SCI Committee of Secrecy (or Correspondence), which emerges as a pivotal factor in the arrests of all the thirteen.

Martin was charged separately. The five other men indicted for high treason with Horne Tooke were:

Thomas Wardle, member of the SCI. See Biographical Index.

Thomas Holcroft, member of the SCI. See Biographical Index.

Matthew Moore, member of the LCS. See Biographical Index. Joseph Moore, a bridle-cutter and saddler's ironmonger, had been arrested by mistake in May and subsequently released, which perhaps accounts for Matthew Moore's continued freedom.

Richard Hodgson, member of the LCS. See Biographical Index. Not to be confused with Edward Hodson.

John Baxter, member of the LCS. See Biographical Index. Not arrested and committed to Newgate till July.

[14] This is probably William Hunter, the officer who received the warrant for Horne Tooke and the others to be committed to the Tower and who presumably escorted them there (PRO PC 2/140, warrant, 19 May 1794).

David Kinghorn was the gaoler assigned to Horne Tooke. He features prominently in the diary. His official title, 'Gentleman Gaoler', was one that Horne Tooke did not feel was justified in the light of Kinghorn's ungentlemanly treatment of him. See JHT's diary entry for 30 May.

[15] Henry Dundas: see Biographical Index; William Wyndham, 1st Baron Grenville, in 1794 secretary of state for the Foreign Department: see Biographical Index; George Grenville-Nugent-Temple, 1st marquis of Buckingham (1753–1813); Jeffrey Amherst, 1st Baron Amherst (1717–1797); John Jeffreys Pratt, 2nd Earl Camden (1759–1840); Granville Leveson Gower, 1st marquis of Stafford (1721–1805), lord privy seal; the chancellor was

Alexander Wedderburn, Lord Loughborough, later (1801) earl of Rosslyn (1733–1805).

Those members of the Privy Council officially recorded as present were: lord chancellor (Loughborough); lord privy seal (Stafford); duke of Montrose; marquis of Buckingham; Earl Camden (Bayham); earl of Chatham; Viscount Sydney; Lord Grenville; Lord Amherst; Lord Auckland; Mr. Secretary Dundas; Sylvester Douglas Esq. (later Lord Glenbervie). Thus Horne Tooke's 'two others or three others' are Montrose, Chatham, Sydney, Auckland, and Douglas.

Reeves, Fawkener, and Ford are not indicated in the official record. William Fawkener (see Biographical Index), as clerk to the Privy Council, was presumably supervising the record-taking; Richard Ford, a Bow Street magistrate, was employed by the Home Department to monitor reformist agitators and handle French agents; see Biographical Index. John Reeves's function there is uncertain; for discussion see Biographical Index.

Perhaps significantly, in view of Horne Tooke's political connection with him in the 1780s, Pitt, who was present at many of the Privy Council examinations, was not present at Horne Tooke's.

[16] The figures refer to the supposed official incomes of the privy councillors who examined JHT. At the top end of the scale Horne Tooke's estimates seem rather exaggerated. Dundas, as secretary of state, treasurer to the navy, president of the Board of Control, and holder of various Scottish perquisites, had perhaps £13,000; Lord Grenville, as secretary of state and auditor of the exchequer, rather less than £10,000. But at the other end it is possible that Horne Tooke underestimated the incomes of Buckingham at £7,000 and of Camden at £6,000; in 1812 their sinecure posts as tellers of the exchequer were each worth £24,000 p.a.

[17] Felix Vaughan, a young barrister and close friend (some say his son or nephew). See n.57 and Biographical Index.

[18] Presumably Captain George Bruhl, Coldstream Regiment of Foot Guards (*A List of the Officers of the Army and Marines with an index; . . .* , forty-third edn. (War Office, 1795).

[19] One of the warders at the Tower: Horne Tooke was initially confined in Burford's lodgings but after three days was removed to the lodgings of another warder, Mold or Mould.

[20] This was secured by Colonel Yorke, deputy lieutenant of the Tower (see n. 46), who informed the Privy Council on 24 May that three of the prisoners were without the means to support themselves in the Tower. The usual sum allowed, he said, was thirteen shillings and sixpence per week. The three were named as Joyce, Thelwall, and Lovett (PRO PC 2/140). Yorke seems simply to have been getting a rubber-stamp endorsement for the payment, which was, as Horne Tooke's entry for 24 May indicates, already understood by the prisoners to be forthcoming.

[21] The payment to Nicholson seems to have been for Horne Tooke's meals, the

payments to Burford and later to Mould apparently being only for lodging.

[22] Count Alvise P. Zenobio was a member of the SCI and a personal friend and correspondent of Horne Tooke, writing to him in 1789 of the glories of the French Revolution, a point taken up by the treasury solicitor in preparing the prosecution (PRO TS 11/951/3495 fo. 80. 'Index to Papers found at John Horne Tooke's Wimbledon'). Zenobio was described by Stephens as the 'representative of a noble Venetian family' (Alexander Stephens, op. cit. (note 5), II, p. 329).

In February 1794 Zenobio had been ordered to quit the country as an undesirable alien (presumably under the provision of the Aliens Act, 33 Geo. III c. 4). To prevent this, Horne Tooke, knowing that he could not be deported while owing money, used the ploy of having him arrested for debt. Later, in June, a libel suit, Count Zenobio v. Axtell, came to court arguing that a report (in French) in the *Courier de Londres* (later *Courier de l'Europe*) of 31 January, which stated that Zenobio had received an order to quit England and which referred to him as 'an adventurer, a *great gambler, who calls himself* Count Zenobio', had damaged his credibility among his creditors (*Morning Post* 23 June 1794 p. 3a, and 28 June 1794 p. 2d). It is difficult to know whether this was also part of the ploy.

Samuel Hood, 1st Lord Hood (1724–1816), an admiral and an Irish peer, had been elected MP for Westminster in 1785. On being appointed a lord of the Admiralty in 1788 he had to stand for re-election. Horne Tooke was prominent amongst his supporters but he lost to Fox's friend Lord John Townshend. His twenty pounds was either an IOU or a banknote, which in those days would have had the physical appearance of short letter. This is why Ford had to scrutinize it carefully.

[23] The magistrate Richard Ford (see Biographical Index) was given permission on 26 May 'from time to time' to visit Horne Tooke in the Tower; the letter, signed by Fawkener, giving him Dundas's authority to take custody of Horne Tooke's keys was also signed on 26 May (PRO PC 2/140).

The heavy scribbling-over and crossing-out of the two words before 'Convention' may have been motivated by the need for secrecy. The Scottish general convention of the delegates from the societies of the Friends of the People (or British Convention) of December 1793 had grown out of the previous general conventions of Scottish societies from December 1792 onwards, on account of which Thomas Muir and Thomas Fyshe Palmer had already been prosecuted and sentenced to transportation for sedition. The British Convention's Scottish secretary, William Skirving, and LCS delegates, Maurice Margarot and Joseph Gerrald, had all been prosecuted on sedition and conspiracy charges and convicted with savage sentences by March 1794, and the SCI's delegate, Charles Sinclair (son of Sir John), was on bail awaiting similar charges (eventually dropped). It was indeed upon the possibility of such a convention being called in London that the crown based its case of high treason, arguing that such a convention, modelled on the national convention in

France, would by construction 'compass or imagine the death of the King'; Sir James Eyre, the chief justice presiding over the trial, added for good measure 'and not only his death but the death and destruction of all order, religion, laws, all property, all security for the lives and liberties of the King's subjects' (*The Trial of Mr. Thomas Hardy for High Treason: containing the whole of the proceedings . . . and the bills of indictment found against Thomas Hardy, John Horne Tooke, John Augustus Bonney* [and others] . . . *Accurately taken in short-hand by Manoah Sibley* (Dublin, 1794), p. 18). The indictment itself also specifically accused the defendants of conspiring to 'cause and procure a Convention and Meeting . . . with intent . . . [to] . . . subvert and alter . . . the legislature, rule and government . . . '.

[24] On 26 May Yorke attended the Privy Council and presented it with a 'return of the Strong Apartments in the different Towers of London': two apartments in the south-east tower, two in the south tower, two in the west tower, and two in the tower on the parade. Yorke was directed to take care that the prisoners 'be removed from the Apartments where they are now confined, to some or other of the Apartments before mentioned' (PRO PC 2/140). From Horne Tooke's later references to the parade it is possible that he was in the tower on the parade, although from another diary entry (20 July) it is clear that he had a good view of the Thames, which would suggest a southerly position. He was directly above Kyd (12 June) and probably a neighbour of Bonney.

[25] I.e., commode, chamber-pot concealed in a heavy-bodied chair.

[26] Vicary Gibbs was, along with Thomas Erskine, Horne Tooke's counsel. 'N.B. GIBBS' may have been added to the 27 May entry as an afterthought. JHT is perhaps making the point here that, contrary to the newspaper report, he had not at this stage seen Gibbs, his counsel. See Biographical Index for both Gibbs and Erskine.

[27] William Cowper (1731–1800), the poet. Horne Tooke evidently treasured this letter as a literary memento of perhaps the most celebrated English poet of the era. No letter of Cowper's to Horne Tooke appears to be extant (cf. James King and Charles Ryskamp (eds.), *The Letters and Prose Writings of William Cowper*, 5 vols. (Oxford, 1979–1986)). Cowper was not a reformer but was nevertheless one of those who initially saw much to celebrate in the French Revolution. Perhaps this was the subject of the letter.

[28] Presumably the letter of 3 June 1793, addressed to Horne Tooke and signed 'Regulus', which discusses the need to call a convention in London to preserve the benefits of 1688 and which refers to 'the scandalous prostitution of Honours and Emoluments by the Crown' and 'insatiable peculation' (PRO TS 11/951/3495).

[29] Horne Tooke worked for Sir Robert Bernard (1740–89) in Huntingdon from 1778–84 both as a political agent and as his estate accountant. Bernard was one of the founding members of JHT's Society for the Support of the Bill of Rights (Alexander Stephens, op. cit. (note 5), I, p. 163). For Sir Robert's

involvement with that society, and for his involvement and final break with Wilkes, see L. B. Namier and J. Brooke (eds.), *The History of Parliament: the House of Commons, 1754–1790*, 3 vols. (London, 1964), II, pp. 86–87. JHT broke with Bernard after an unpleasant altercation over JHT's handling of Bernard's financial affairs.

[30] John Frost, attorney and prominent member of the SCI. He was examined before the Privy Council on 31 May on suspicion of treasonable practices but discharged (PRO PC 2/140). He had been imprisoned for six months, pilloried, and struck off the roll of attorneys the previous year for saying, whilst drunk in a coffee house, that he was for 'equality and no king'. See Biographical Index.

[31] John Williams, member of both the SCI and the LCS. The *Morning Post* of 3 June noted that he had been charged with seditious practices and had seven children under the age of 10 (p. 2d), and the issue of 4 June reported that he was in the custody of a messenger in a hotel in Parliament Street and that he was 'suffered [as] he pleases, to converse in private with his friends' (p. 2d). Williams was examined by the Privy Council several times. The record of the interview of 11 June reveals a rather over-anxious man with an inclination to allow words to be put into his mouth by his interlocutors. Although he categorically denied hearing any talk of arming with pikes, he let himself say that he had seen a 'knife of a particular construction' at Hardy's house. (See also n. 64 for Williams's recantation.)

It would seem that the crown was particularly interested in Hardy's bread-and cheese-knives (see PRO TS 11/3502/1 fo. 41 and PRO PC 2/140 fo. 186, printed pagination 96; also 'The Trial of Thomas Hardy for High Treason', in T. B. and T. J. Howell (compilers), op. cit. (note 5), XXIV (34 & 35 George III . . . A.D. 1794) (London, 1818), col. 744, for the knives). The prosecution was attempting to gain evidence of armed insurrection and, in this connection, pressed a number of persons, especially John Hillier, Philip Franklow, and a nineteen-year-old silversmith, John Edwards.

[32] Prior to this, Hardy had been held in the custody of Gurnell and Lauzun in King Street.

The five mentioned by JHT as being sent to Newgate but not named by him were John Ashley (shoemaker), Richard Hayward, Jean Baptist Russell (anglicized from Roussel or Roussell), Thomas Spence (the bookseller), and John Hillier (tallow chandler cum bookseller); this had happened on 29 May (PRO TS 11/957/3502/2). Of these John Hillier and John Ashley, along with John Philip Frankloe (or Francklow) (a tailor of China Row, Lambeth), were eventually indicted for high treason. They were all members of the LCS.

By 29 May 1794 there were twenty-three persons listed as having been taken into custody (PRO TS 11/957/3502/2); cf. Clive Emsley, 'Repression, "terror" and the rule of law in England during the decade of the French Revolution', *English Historical Review*, 100 (1985), 801–25, at p. 809. But this list is not necessarily accurate and, in any case, does not count those on bail like the wine merchant, John Williams, the law student, John Pearson, the engraver, William Sharp, and the lawyer, Christopher Hull; although it does mention Kyd, who was then still on bail. Nor does it list those who had not been apprehended like Wardle, Moore, and Hodgson; or Holcroft, who at this stage did not even know he was under suspicion, although he was eventually to be named as one of the twelve against whom a true bill of indictment for high treason was found (Thomas Holcroft, op. cit. (note 13), pp. 24–29).

[33] Lieutenant-General James Murray (1734–94). His nephew was the 4th duke of Atholl, in whose interest he was elected MP for Perthshire in 1790 (R. G. Thorne (ed.), *The History of Parliament: the House of Commons 1790–1820*, 5 vols. (London, 1986), IV, p. 645).

[34] This was in 1777, when he was prosecuted for libel for accusing British soldiers of murdering protestors at Lexington and Concord (Massachusetts) in 1775 in an advertisement to raise money for the victims' relatives. JHT indicates that the prosecution cost him £1,200 (23 May 104/05r).

[35] His 'Boy' is presumably his illegitimate son, referred to by Stephens, op. cit. (note 5), only as 'Mr Montague'; he sojourned at Cambridge briefly before a scandal necessitated his departure for India in the service of the East India Company. In a letter to Horne Tooke dated 12 August 1789 Count Zenobio mentions the arrival of JHT's son in Madras (PRO TS 11/951/3495). Samuel Rogers relates, however, that JHT virtually disowned his son when he returned from India after being dismissed from some military situation for misconduct. He subsequently joined the dragoons as a private, an act which JHT considered a 'catastrophe' (G. H. Powell (ed.), op. cit. (note 2), pp. 99–100). It is unknown whether, like Coleridge in similar circumstances in 1794, he had his discharge subsequently purchased by his family. But none of this explains what happened to JHT's 'Boy' when his father was in the King's Bench prison in 1777.

Horne Tooke's 'Girls' are his two illegitimate daughters Mary and Charlotte Hart. JHT made no secret of his paternity, and his genuine concern for them during his period in the Tower is very apparent. The girls were not without their usefulness. Charlotte, who 'had acquired as much Latin as most of the bishops', and Mary, who 'possessed an excellent understanding', between them managed household affairs and 'were accustomed, at times, to act in the capacity of his secretary and amanuensis' (Alexander Stephens, op. cit. (note 5), II, pp. 162–64). Their maternal origins are unknown. But one of Horne Tooke's livelier *bons mots*, often quoted as an example of his wit (e.g. in R. G. Thorne (ed.), op. cit (note 33)), may well have had some bearing upon his family circumstances. In response to a friend's suggestion that he should take a wife, JHT is supposed to have replied 'With all my heart; whose wife shall it be?' (John Cam Hobhouse, Lord Broughton, *Recollections of a Long Life*, ed. Lady Dorchester (Lord Broughton's daughter), 6 vols. (London, 1909), I, p. 38). Before the advent of nineteenth-century codes of sexual propriety it was not considered disgraceful for a man to have illegitimate children provided he paid for their upkeep. It was more usual, however, for such children to live with their mother along with the children of her official family or to be farmed out to a boarding school. Indeed Stephens tells us that initially the eldest (Mary) had been 'placed at a respectable boarding school, at a little distance from town'. JHT first saw her when he moved to Richmond Buildings in Soho (1788), when she was already a 'young lady' and came for the holidays. The younger child, Charlotte, subsequently joined her and the arrangement seems eventually to have become permanent (Alexander Stephens, op. cit. (note 5), II, p. 28). This holiday arrangement may have occurred upon the death of a putative Mr. Hart: in his prison diary JHT records payments not only to 'M.ʳˢ. Hart' (2 June) but to 'Hart' as well (e.g., 2 June, 8 July, and 20 September). But the two forms probably both refer to Mrs. Hart. In 1796 the ministerial press made some very unpleasant references to JHT's domestic arrangements (*Sun*, 9 June; *True Briton*, 12 June).

[36] This was possibly the Asylum for Female Orphans in Lambeth. JHT's father, John Horne, had been a liberal subscriber and founding treasurer of the Middlesex Hospital and JHT may have been following in his footsteps as a patron of charities.

[37] The first time was on 23 May at Burford's where he was lodged before he was moved to Mould's. In both cases it would seem that it took the authorities four days to organize workmen to instal the bars.

[38] See n. 13.

[39] Francis Vernon (?1715–83), first earl of Shipbrook in the Irish peerage. General Charles Vernon was lieutenant of the Tower (see n. 82). The 'Yeoman Porter', in fact deputy yeoman porter, was one Louis Grauz/Groz/Gruaz, who appears to have earned Horne Tooke's ire: see diary entries for 24 and 25 August. JHT fluctuates between Grauz and Gruaz as his preferred spelling.

[40] Horne Tooke's sister, Mary, married Thomas Wildman, wine merchant and friend of Wilkes. JHT's nephew, John, is presumably their son.

[41] Presumably the mother of his two girls. See n. 35.

[42] William Tooke, Horne Tooke's friend and patron whose name he adopted. See Biographical Index.

[43] First Marquis Cornwallis, constable of the Tower. See n. 82.

[44] Frederick Cornwallis, D.D., archbishop of Canterbury, who lived from 1713 until 1783.

[45] A sieve is a basket containing half a bushel used, for example, at the vegetable market at Covent Garden. Presumably a 'halfsieve' contained a quarter of a bushel.

[46] Colonel John Yorke (? –1826), deputy lieutenant of the Tower of London. See *DNB* entry for his son, Sir Charles Yorke (1790–1880), field-marshal.

[47] On 5 June (PRO PC 2/140).

[48] As Bonney's brother-in-law, he was probably the Thomas Hague, attorney, listed in John Browne, *Browne's General Law List, . . .* , 16th edn. (London,

1797), of Dorset Court, Cannon Row, Westminster. Hague had earlier been permitted to visit Bonney by the authority of the Privy Council on 19 May (PRO PC 2/140).

[49] This decision does not appear to have been a special case. On 4 June, owing, it would appear, to complaints from the Tower authorities about the inconvenience of so many visitors, all visit permits, apart from those of spouses (or close relatives) — and they were curtailed to a maximum of two a week — were revoked (PRO PC 2/140). Kinghorn applied for and received from the Privy Council an assistant gaoler (Wallace) to cope with the rather novel circumstances occasioned by the sudden influx of state prisoners; obviously the system was under strain.

[50] The *True Briton*, like the *Sun*, was established with direct government backing; the *World*, *Herald*, *Oracle*, and *The Times* were subsidized by the government. Others, like the *Morning Chronicle*, *Morning Post*, and *Gazetteer*, were opposition oriented. (See A. Aspinall, *Politics and the Press c. 1780–1850* (London, 1949), pp. 68, 78.)

[51] The advertisement consisted of resolutions of the general committee of the LCS, 5 June 1794. See British Library, shelf mark 8138 n. i. (101).

[52] William Ross and George Higgins, His Majesty's messengers in ordinary. Ross had had custody of Joyce prior to his committal to the Tower.

[53] William Sharp, the engraver, member of the SCI and close personal friend of Horne Tooke. See Biographical Index.

[54] Christopher Hull, barrister, and member of the SCI; he was treasurer in 1792 to the Fund for Assisting the French in the Cause of Freedom, his own donation being recorded as £50 (SCI papers: PRO TS 11/951/3493 and 3495). The *Morning Post* of 30 May 1794, referring to him as a reputable and eminent attorney in Paper Buildings, Temple, reported that he had been taken into custody the previous evening (p. 3c). On 6 June the paper noted that he had undergone his examination before the Privy Council and had been liberated 'in the most respectable manner' (p. 3b). According to his testimony before the Privy Council on 30 May (PRO PC 2/140) he apparently had regretted his role as treasurer to the fund, had resigned from it, paying back all the money, and had not in fact made any contribution himself. When asked how he could have been induced to belong to the SCI, he said he really did not know — he differed so much with them in politics — he had been introduced — and at the time there had been respectable characters belonging to it. He claimed that he had been 'cut' by the SCI because he had refused to put up bail for Frost in 1793, and that Horne Tooke did not trust him; and he made much of his own low opinion of Horne Tooke.

[55] A reminder of the curious social norms of this period. Ross seems to have wished merely to pay Horne Tooke a courtesy visit, just as Dundas was later to pay the journalist John Binns a courtesy visit in 1800, when he was being held without charge in Gloucester gaol. On that occasion Dundas was accompanied by his youthful second wife, Lady Jane, and his two grown-up daugh-

ters (see Binns, op. cit. (note 9), p. 140). As a messenger of state presumably Ross had some influence. Horne Tooke is probably suggesting, however, that Kinghorn blocked the visit out of petty officiousness. It should be noted that all visits to the prisoners in the Tower, at least at this early stage, even that of magistrate Richard Ford, had to be authorized by the Privy Council. (See PRO, PC 2/140 *passim*. For Ford's authority see fo. 216, printed pagination 111.)

[56] The Habeas Corpus Suspension Act. See n. 11.

[57] Vaughan was junior counsel to Gibbs and Erskine for the trials and was counsel for Martin, but that was only one of the reasons he 'excused himself' from being examined by the Privy Council. The chief one was the fact of his close relationship with Horne Tooke.

That with respect to one of the persons who appear to be most particularly aimed at, Mr Horne Tooke, he stood in such a Relation, that it would be highly improper that he should say any Thing with respect to him. – That from his constant and early care and affection for him, he had been used to consider him a Father from his Infancy, and that under those Circumstances he was persuaded Their Lordships would not press him on the subject.

His qualms seems to have been respected. He was requested to withdraw (5 June: PRO PC 2/140). See Biographical Index for a discussion of Vaughan's relationship to Horne Tooke.

[58] Dr. George Pearson, physician, chemist, and non-political friend of Horne Tooke; see Biographical Index.

Henry Cline, surgeon and friend of Horne Tooke; see Biographical Index. *DNB* states that Cline was surgeon at St. Thomas's Hospital, as do [Peter Barfoot and John Wilkes (compilers)], *The Universal British Directory of Trade, Commerce, and Manufacture . . .* (London, 1793), p. 461. Horne Tooke seems therefore to have been mistaken in later stating he was at Guy's (see diary entry, 10 June, letter of 9 June to Mr. Fawkener, secretary to the Privy Council).

[59] Certainly no such dialogue is recorded in the Privy Council Register. It is possible that newspapers may have circulated it; some did occasionally carry supposedly verbatim accounts of the Privy Council examinations. Or it may have come to him on the grapevine within the Tower itself. Vaughan's role, as far as the crown was concerned at that stage, was as a witness to the address of the London Corresponding Society to the societies of Great Britain of 29 November 1792 (a piece of prosecution evidence) and as witness to a letter from the Norwich Constitutional Society of 15 April 1793 (another piece of prosecution evidence) (See PRO TS 11/957/3502/2, 'Points to be proved . . . and names of witnesses by whom they are to be proved'). He quite obviously could have supplied a great deal more personal information. Perhaps he was spared on account of the frail state of his health or because the prosecution had already fixed upon William Sharp, the engraver and intimate friend of Horne Tooke, as their chief source of information. The fact that Vaughan, although a

member of the LCS, was never a member of the SCI probably also weakened his potential usefulness as a witness.

[60] There were two reports to the House of Commons by its Committee of Secrecy in this period: the first was on 17 May, and the other on 6 June 1794. There were also two reports by a Committee of Secrecy of the House of Lords. See JHT's reference to the second House of Commons Report (12 June). It was the House of Commons reports which were the most substantial and significant, containing as they did transcripts of the records of the societies and other documents which were later to be used in evidence.

The House of Commons's Committee of Secrecy was set up on 13 May following the first arrests in order to establish a basis for action against those arrested. It was more than somewhat skewed in favour of the government, including, as it did, Pitt, Dundas, the attorney general (Sir John Scott), the solicitor general (Sir John Mitford), the lord advocate of Scotland (Dundas's nephew Robert Dundas), and Edmund Burke. For a full list of the committee see *Journals of the House of Commons*, XLIX (21 January–25 November 1794), p. 594 (14 May 1794).

[61] See n. 10 for an account of Horne Tooke's speech to the Privy Council.

[62] Presumably the Habeas Corpus Suspension Act. See n. 11.

[63] Scirrhus — a hard tumour, possibly an early stage of cancer. From Stephens, though, we learn that this was diagnosed by his physician as a 'hydrocele', in the treatment of which he was recommended, rather than undergoing surgery, to take the chance of its disappearing spontaneously; something which actually occurred a few years before his death (Alexander Stephens, op. cit. (note 5), II, p. 423). See n. 77 for further details of Horne Tooke's physical ailments.

[64] Whatever Horne Tooke's source for this information, what he evidently did not know was that John Williams, at his examination of the 6 June, had submitted a written statement declaring that he would forthwith 'withdraw myself from all political societies whatever and regulate my Conduct as to give no cause for suspicion in future'. He was nevertheless interrogated again, as was his brother, George Williams, a leather seller (PRO PC 2/140).

[65] John Pearce, clerk to Martin, was deputy or sub-secretary to the LCS (elected secretary after Hardy's arrest). He was examined by the Privy Council on 23 May and 2 June. From the official record it would seem that the Privy Council was more interested in whether Pearce had seen Hardy's bread- and cheese-knives than in Martin's affairs (PRO PC 2/140). He does not seem to have been sent to Newgate, being remanded on bail on 8 July with a recognizance of £1,000 and one surety of £500.

This is the John Pearce who stated at the special-commission hearing of 2 October that he was Mr. Martin's articled clerk and sought permission to attend him in prison, and who was noted by the court as himself liable to be charged (*The Trial of Mr. Thomas Hardy* . . . op. cit. (note 23), p. 46; see also G. H. Powell (ed.), op. cit. (note 2), p. 121).

[66] Horne Tooke was apparently writing this with knowledge of what subse-

quently happened, as explained in the next entry, concerning his toast and conversation with the warder, Dixon. He may have been in the habit of writing two or more days' diary in one session.

[67] W. Shakespeare, *Measure for Measure* IV. ii. 82–83:

[Exit Provost]

Duke: This is a gentle provost; seldom when
            The Steeled gaoler is the friend of men.

See also the diary entry for 3 August: ' "It is a gentle Jailor." and, a <u>wise</u> one'.

[68] The 'address to the foot of the throne' was apropos of the Report of the Secret Committee and was proposed by Lord Grenville (foreign secretary) to the House of Lords on 13 June. In his speech recommending such an address, Grenville spoke of a 'cool, deliberate, systematic plan to destroy the constitution of England, and to substitute in its place the tyranny of France'.

On 16 June Pitt, recommending the address to the House of Commons, spoke of 'a systematic design, deliberately formed and long acted upon, directed to the subversion of the British constitution'. He spoke of the planned convention, which would embody Barère's doctrine of the right of the people to be in a sovereign state of insurrection, with 'the sacred duty of subverting established governments' (W. Cobbett (ed.), *The Parliamentary History of England from the Earliest Period to the Year 1803*, 36 vols. (London, 1806–20), XXXI (1818), cols. 909–10, 915).

[69] Sir James Eyre; see Biographical Index.

[70] Arthur Brice, lieutenant, Coldstream Guards.

[71] Charles Stanhope, 3rd Earl Stanhope (1753–1815). A champion of the French Revolution, known and addressed as 'Citizen Stanhope'; see Biographical Index.

[72] Members of Trinity House Corporation, an ancient association of English mariners. Given its first charter by Henry VIII in 1514, it subsequently received powers to raise tolls for the upkeep of coast lights. It is still today the national lighthouse authority for England and Wales as well as the U.K. Pilotage Authority. Until 1795 its headquarters were in Deptford. William Pitt was its master and Lord Chancellor Loughborough an elder brother.

[73] Thomas Thompson (1767–1818), MP for Evesham and member of the SCI.

[74] A term for testicles, now only colloquial.

[75] Presumably a medication; see also n. 77.

[76] The *True Briton* like the *Sun* was a government newspaper and unlikely to be subtle in its attack upon opposition principles. We were unable to identify this particular issue, but the tone of the piece Horne Tooke complains of here may be imagined if it was in a similar vein to other songs published by that newspaper. Here is 'To Quacks and Reformers' of 5 July 1794.

> Last week, aged *fifty-four* Fame tells us,
>   Th'*immortal* GRAHAM crossed the Styx, Sir;
> Of old th'*immortal* PARACELSUS
>   Reach'd *thirty-five* with his *Elixir*.
>
> Would you, from past and present movements,
>   Ask the prophetic Muse to tell
> Th'event of our *Quack State-improvements*,
>   And when *they* also lead to Hell:
>
> She answers — In their proper season,
>   Rich crimes as rich Rewards will claim;
> And whether folks are hang'd for Treason
>   This year or next, 'tis much the same.

Note: James Graham (1745–94) was a renowned medical practitioner, some of whose ideas on hygiene and exercise have since become accepted. See *DNB*. He died in June 1794. Paracelsus is presumably Theophrastus Bombastus von Hohenheim (1493–1541), long famous as a medical practitioner but more recently recognized as a pioneer of modern chemistry.

[77] A thin tube, generally of waxed linen, for dilating or medicating the rectum or other bodily apertures. This event is recorded virtually on a daily basis throughout JHT's time in the Tower from mid-June onwards. From Stephens we learn that, while still a schoolboy, Horne Tooke suffered from a 'complaint of the rectum, which continued during the whole of his life', consisting of 'a difficulty of performing one of the functions of nature, which obliged him to have recourse to a peculiar management, in order to transact business without interruption, or engage in the usual amusements of life' (Alexander Stephens, op. cit. (note 5), II, pp. 420–21). It is perhaps remarkable then that JHT was able to do without Mr. Cline's services till 16 June, when both Pearson and Cline first visited him. The first mention of Mr. Cline's 'passing a bougie' is not till 21 June. It is possible though, notwithstanding Stephens's evidence, that the bougie was used to treat his testicular rather than his intestinal condition.

[78] Sharp would have been well aware of Pitt's association with the SCI and of his previous activities on behalf of reform, which may have been the basis of the quarrel. There seems, however, to have been some confusion as to who actually uttered the words in inverted commas in the text. Philip A. Brown, op. cit. (note 9), p. 122, says that Sharp reported that it was Pitt, not Reeves. The Privy Council Register records only that at the end of Sharp's examination of 6 June:

It was then recommended to him to come the next time to the Board with a Resolution to speak the whole Truth, fairly openly and candidly — not disguising and endeavouring to mislead by giving colour to Words, as he had just done in expressing his approbation of Ca Ira [a revolutionary song sung at the SCI dinner at the Crown and Anchor on 2 May], as if it was a Question of Music and not of political Sentiment . . .

PRO PC 2/140 p. 316, stamped p. 161

[79] A member of the SCI, Arthur Blake was examined by the Privy Council on 14 June probably because he was a steward at the SCI dinner at the Crown and Anchor of 2 May at which republican songs and toasts were a feature. He subsequently wrote a letter (published on 24 June) to the editor of the *Morning Chronicle* apparently in response to insults and misinterpretations in the ministerial papers. It was his final paragraph which no doubt Horne Tooke considered 'Honest'.

My conduct either as a Member of the Constitutional Society, or as an Englishman and *a true friend to my Country*, has been such as to bid defiance to the most calumniating tongue; and I trust the Privy Council are convinced by the *investigations they have thought proper to call for, that my principles* are yet *unstained*. But to persevere in a *legal way*, until a Parliamentary Reform is obtained I here pledge myself *I will*; and as far as I know of the Constitutional Society, I believe their object to have been nothing more.

[80] *Morning Post* Wednesday 25 June 1794, pp. 3c–4a–b. A lengthy letter to the editor attacking the sinecure system.

[81] With some justification Horne Tooke was convinced that Reeves's 'employers' were the ministry (see Reeves, John, in Biographical Index), whose object of monitoring and suppressing dissident sentiment in the country Reeves's loyalist or alarmist associations actively assisted.

The *Morning Post* of 26 May 1794, p. 2c, remarked that 'nothing can exceed the avidity with which the *Alarmists* examine the papers of those obscure characters who are at present the object of so much political discussion' (i.e. the score or so of persons, including the thirteen charged with high treason).

[82] The constable of the Tower was Charles, 2nd Earl and 1st Marquis Cornwallis (1738–1805). He held this position even while governor general of India although he was in England from February 1794. In 1798 he was created lord lieutenant and commander-in-chief in Ireland.

The lieutenant of the Tower was General Charles Vernon. See John Bayley, op. cit. (note 13), II (1825), pp. 654–67. The terms 'governor' and 'lieutenant-governor' seem to have been interchangeable: cf. [Peter Barfoot and John Wilkes (compilers)], op. cit. (note 58), p. 27, for list of officers of the Tower of London. Horne Tooke made several attempts, in incidental jottings, to work out the hierarchy.

[83] Dundas's only son, Robert Dundas (1771–1851), was returned MP for Hastings on 9 May 1794; Dundas's nephew, William Dundas (1762–1845), was returned MP for Anstruther Burghs on 1 July 1794 through the influence of his uncle (R. G. Thorne (ed.), op. cit. (note 33), III, pp. 647 and 653).

[84] George Wood (1743–1824), barrister engaged by the crown in drafting the indictment. He entered parliament in 1796 and was knighted in 1807. The attorney general was Sir John Scott.

[85] Thomas Keate. (1745–1821), surgeon at St. George's Hospital from 1792; surgeon to the army in 1793; later surgeon to the prince of Wales (*DNB*).

[86] By filing an information the crown could circumvent the requirement for a grand jury on the basis of a common-law action by the king through his attorney general in the Court of the King's Bench. Speed of prosecution was the main advantage. Of course, as Horne Tooke would have been well aware, it was a legal process historically associated with the Star Chamber and other forms of state oppression, although a fairly common procedure without sinister significance by the late eighteenth century. Bacon defines an information as follows:

An information may be defined an accusation or complaint exhibited against a person for some criminal offence . . . , either immediately against the king, or against a private person, which, from its enormity or dangerous tendency, the publick good requires should be restrained and punished, and differs principally from an indictment in this, that an indictment is an accusation found by the oath of twelve men, whereas an information is only the allegation of the officer who exhibits it.

> Matthew Bacon, *A New Abridgement of the Law. The Seventh Edition, Corrected; with large additions, including the latest statutes and authorities*, 8 vols. (London, 1832), vols. II, III, and IV (except the addenda) by Sir Henry Gwilliam, vols. I, V, VI, VII, and VIII, and the addenda to the other volumes by Charles Edward Dodd, IV, p. 402.

George Wood (1743–1824) was one of the barristers acting for the crown.

[87] The allies were driven out of the western part of the Austrian Netherlands (now Belgium) in the first week of July 1794.

[88] Thomas Walker (1749–1817), cotton merchant, and founder and president of the Manchester Constitutional Society. He was acquitted of conspiracy at his trial in Manchester in April 1794 when he was defended by Thomas Erskine and Felix Vaughan.

The king's speech of the previous day, winding up the session of parliament, had commented on 'designs that have been formed against the government and constitution of these kingdoms . . . against our domestic happiness [and which] are essentially connected with the system now prevalent in France, of which the principles and spirit are irreconcilably hostile to all regular and established government . . . ' (W. Cobbett (ed.), op. cit. (note 68), XXXI (1818), col. 958).

That Horne Tooke was making any connection between the king's speech and Walker's trial is unlikely. The transcript of Walker's trial of April may have just been published.

[89] Presumably Dr. James Beattie (1735–1803), Scottish poet, essayist, moral philosopher, and fellow philologist. His *Essay on the Nature and Immutability of Truth, . . .* (London, 1770) was listed in Horne Tooke's library on his death ([John Horne Tooke], *Books. A catalogue of the valuable library, late the*

property of J. Horne Tooke [London, 1813], items 44, 45). Horne Tooke's two finger-arrows are definitely pointing to the *Gil Blas* excerpt, a fact suggesting either some profound significance, now lost, or simply that he wanted to jog his memory at some future date to pass the excerpt on to Dr. Beattie.

90 *Gil Blas*, a picaresque novel (1715) by Alain-René Le Sage. This work went through many English editions in different translations.

Rogers quotes Horne Tooke as saying that he read *Gil Blas* in the Tower as well as *Tom Jones* and 'some other novels a wardour's wife lent me' (probably Mrs. Mould, with whom he seems to have been on good terms): G. H. Powell (ed.), op. cit. (note 2), p. 96.

91 Dundas's property was adjacent to Horne Tooke's at Wimbledon. This meeting of Pitt, Dundas, and others was possibly the occasion at which the details of the imminent coalition ministry were thrashed out. Pitt was apparently unhappy about the prospect of handing over the Home Department to Portland since he and Dundas operated, as he said, 'like one'. On the 5 July he wrote to Lord Grenville begging him to let him offer Portland Grenville's job of foreign secretary instead. Would Grenville acquiesce? Would he please meet him at Wimbledon (where Pitt was to dine that evening) for breakfast tomorrow? In 'this heat' the earlier the better (*Historical Manuscripts Commission 30; Fourteenth Report, Appendix, Part V. The Manuscripts of J. B. Fortescue, Esq., preserved at Dropmore*, 10 vols. (London, 1892–97), II (1895), pp. 595–96). As it turned out Portland declined the Foreign Department and Pitt resigned himself to having a new home secretary. Whether knowledge of these goings on at Wimbledon would have mitigated Horne Tooke's sense of martyrdom is doubtful.

92 Later (10 September), at the foot of a copy of a letter to John Macnamara, he repeats and extends the quotation to include a second line: 'For thee, fair freedom, welcome even the last'. Horne Tooke wrote some patriotic poems himself from the 1760s on; perhaps this is from one of them. In November 1796 at the Crown and Anchor a Mr. Rukin sang a song on a similar theme, the words of which appear to have been written by Horne Tooke (someone has written his name on the bottom of it) and which begins:

> Rouse, arouse from this slumber, thou child of Oppression;
> Away with this vile, this unmanly depression

and ends:

> And be this our decision, whilst FREEDOM survives,
> That the day of its death be the LAST OF OUR LIVES.

> British Library, C. 60. m. 6, John Horne Tooke, [A collection of
> pamphlets and single sheets . . .] [1778–1812], II (15).

Terrible stuff for a man who prided himself on having read every dramatic masterpiece in every language known to him (G. H. Powell (ed.), op. cit. (note 2), p. 96). Nor was he content with leaving the performance to others. His apparently less-than-musical renditions at SCI dinners were of some interest to the Privy Council (PRO PC 2/140 *passim*) and were noted in evidence at the trial of Thomas Hardy (T. B. and T. J. Howell (compilers), op. cit. (note 5), XXIV (34 & 35 George III . . . A.D. 1794) (London, 1818), col. 751). In his library was a collection of patriotic songs ([Anon.], *Songs Patriotic* (London, 1793)), but whether of his own composition is unlikely ([John Horne Tooke], op. cit. (note 89)).

93 Presumably Charles Hamerton, 'paviour', one of the two sheriffs of London in 1794 (*A London Directory* . . . (London, printed for W. Lowndes, [1794]), p. 3). He was mentioned by Horne Tooke, in the prepared text of a speech he intended making to the court, as paviour to the Custom House and to the Board of Ordnance and as actively involved in the trials, being responsible, in his capacity as sheriff, for constituting the juries (see also n. 142 for Godwin on the composition of the juries). This speech, which Stephens quotes from in the *Memoirs*, on the advice of JHT's counsel was never delivered or published (Alexander Stephens, op. cit. (note 5), II, p. 137).

94 It would seem that Frost had abused his self-appointed role of protector of Horne Tooke's family. JHT was a very paternalistic employer with rigid standards (see Alexander Stephens, op. cit. (note 5), II, pp. 289–90) but it was his daughters' well-being rather than the virtue of his housemaids which seems to have concerned him most. It was probably this issue that was still troubling JHT more than a month later (see entry for 24 August, when he requested that the gaoler should not be present during an interview with one of his daughters owing to the 'delicate' nature of some family problem. (There is in fact no record of such an interview having actually taken place.) John Frost later continued to be politically involved with the Tooke/Burdett circle. As late as 1802 he was acting as legal adviser to Burdett's successful Middlesex campaign. But eventually he fell out with them and the connection was severed (J. Ann Hone, op. cit. (note 4), p. 93). Perhaps this incident may have had something to do with it. See also Biographical Index.

95 J. Cornwallis is listed as gentleman porter, Tower of London, at a salary of 84*l*.10*s*. in [Peter Barfoot and John Wilkes (compilers)], op. cit. (note 58), p. 27, but the army list for 1794 (*A List of the Officers of the Army and Marines with an index;* . . . , forty-second edn. (War Office, 1794), gives Spencer Madan as gentleman porter; so perhaps Horne Tooke is correct in his identification and J. Cornwallis was the yeoman porter.

96 Horne Tooke subsequently quoted this paragraph almost verbatim in his opening address to the court (T. B. and T. J. Howell (compilers), op. cit. (note 5), XXV (35 & 36 George III . . . A.D. 1794–1796) (London, 1818), col. 73).

97 Possibly Edward Southwall Trotter (Wadham College, Oxford; matriculated 11 October 1790, aged 18), son of Edward Trotter, a doctor, of Co. Down, Ireland (see Joseph Foster, *Alumni Oxonienses: the members of the University of Oxford 1715–1886*, 4 vols. (Oxford, 1887–88), IV (1888)). It is most unlikely that the well-wisher belonged to the more illustrious, government-favoured

'brotherhood of the Trotters', Alexander, John, and Coutts Trotter (see William Jerdan, *The Autobiography of William Jerdan, . . .,* 3 vols. (London, Hall, Virtue and Co., 1852–53), II, pp. 214 ff.).

[98] The Greek title of *The Diversions of Purley.*

[99] Portland replaced Dundas as home secretary when he brought his Whig followers into the government in July 1794 (see n. 91 and Biographical Index). Dundas became secretary of state for war (a new position).

The significance of this remark is unknown, unless Horne Tooke is simply making a comment on Portland's relative humanity compared with Dundas's insensitivity. Certainly Portland seems to have been careful to avoid unnecessary hardship. He apparently rapped the treasury solicitor, Joseph White, over the knuckles in October for confining in prison the Scottish witnesses brought to London for the trial even though he had no intention of prosecuting them (draft letter of apology from Joseph White to the duke of Portland 27 October 1794, PRO TS 11/957/3502/2). JHT is probably referring to George Crawford, who had been secretary of the Glasgow Associated Friends of the People in October 1792 (Henry W. Meikle, *Scotland and the French Revolution* (Glasgow, 1912), p. 92). According to the *Morning Post* of 28 July (p. 3b) he had been intercepted on the road to Harwich having been suspected of carrying dispatches for a national convention 'or of a treasonable nature'.

[100] The State Papers, subsequently preserved in the Public Record Office, were at this time housed in the Tower, in the Record or Wakefield Tower. Horne Tooke's interest may well have been the records of the courts, King's Bench, Common Pleas, and Exchequer, which were housed there as the 'king's treasure'. The keeper of the records at the time would have been Thomas Astle, the author of *The Origin and Progress of Writing . . .* (London, 1784). It is easy to imagine that he and the philologist prisoner might have had a few things in common (see Bayley, op. cit. (note 82), I, pp. 218 f.).

[101] James Adair (?1743–98), king's serjeant, led for the prosecution in the treason trials.

[102] Erasmus Darwin (1731–1802), *Zoonomia, or the Laws of Organic Life,* 2 vols. (London, 1794–96). J. Johnson, the publisher of Darwin's book, was also JHT's publisher.

[103] Possibly Dr. Henry Jerome de Salis (1738–1807), D.D., in 1777 vicar of Wing, Buckinghamshire, chaplain-in-ordinary to the king, count of the Holy Roman Empire. According to John P. De Salis, *The De Salis Family in the British Commonwealth: genealogical tables and short historical notes on past and present members* (Bristol, 1959), Henry Jerome was the son of the 2nd count de Salis and brother of Peter, 3rd count de Salis. He was also from 1774 the rector of St. Antholin, Watling Street, in the City of London, a living which he held concurrently with Wing in Buckinghamshire. There is no evidence that he was a member of the SCI, at least from 1792 to 1794, but he was evidently a sympathizer.

[104] The Crown and Anchor in Arundel Street off the Strand was virtually the

London headquarters of radical activity in the late eighteenth and early nineteenth centuries. Its spacious banqueting room at the back hosted 2,000 radicals for a celebratory dinner (at which Horne Tooke was present) on the occasion of Fox's birthday in 1798. The meeting-place of the SCI from 18 May 1792, it was, however, in November 1792 also the meeting-place of Reeves's Association for the Protection of Liberty and Property against Republicans and Levellers.

[105] 'Quod Vide' means 'Which See', i.e., the text of the motion. This incident was at a grand dinner for 650 people, presided over by Lord Stanhope at the Crown and Anchor, and held under the auspices of the SCI on 14 July 1790 to celebrate the first anniversary of the fall of the Bastille.

As a leading Whig MP, Sheridan was in much less immediate danger of being prosecuted than private citizens like Horne Tooke. At the outset of his political career in the early 1780s Sheridan had been a member (though not an active one) of the SCI. It is a little ironic that Sheridan was a leading member of the gentlemanly Friends of the People, whose aim was to wrest the reform platform out of the hands of supposedly dangerous men like Horne Tooke (L. G. Mitchell, *Charles James Fox and the Disintegration of the Whig Party 1782–1794* (London, 1971), p. 196). Sheridan nevertheless appeared as a witness for Horne Tooke at the 1794 trial.

William Newman, sheriff in 1790, was alderman for Faringdon Within.

[106] Cartwright was of course closely associated with Horne Tooke both politically and personally. The refusal, perhaps more newsworthy since it came from Portland rather than Dundas, prompted a public outcry in the opposition press (see *Morning Post* 2 August 1794, p. 3b). Yet it is hard to believe that John Cartwright (the father of the SCI) actually expected to be admitted to see Horne Tooke. See Biographical Index.

[107] William Bosville (1745–1813), bon-vivant and SCI member.

[108] This was speculation. The press was evidently getting garbled reports and confusing the issuing of a special commission of oyer and terminer in Edinburgh with the high treason trials there. It was not till 4 September that the Privy Council made representation to the king for the issuing of such a special commission in London (PRO PC 2/140). On 18 July the Privy Council had directed that the lord chief justice of the King's Bench, Lord Kenyon, assemble the judges in order to 'take their Opinion' as to what legal procedures should be followed.

The special commission of oyer and terminer eventually opened at the session house, Clerkenwell, on 2 October. Its purpose was 'for enquiring, hearing and determining of all High Treasons and Misprisions of Treasons, in compassing or imagining the death of the King, levying war against his Majesty in the realm, or in adhering to the King's enemies within the realm; or giving them aid or comfort within the said realm or elsewhere' (*The Trial of Mr. Thomas Hardy . . .* op. cit. (note 23), p. 9). It consisted of twenty-two commissioners including seven judges, and a grand jury of twenty-two.

The grand jury was asked to find a true bill against each of the accused so that they could stand trial before a petty jury. No defence evidence could be presented at this stage, and very little prosecution evidence either, although it could be demanded (see John S. James, *Stroud's Judicial Dictionary of Words and Phrases*, 5 vols., 4th edn. (London, 1972), II, p. 1186, and V, p. 2832; Thomas Edlyne Tomlins, *The Law-Dictionary . . .* , 2 vols. 4th edn. (London, 1835), II, no pagination, s.v. Special Commission).

[109] John Chatfield, member of the SCI. A timber merchant of Hatton Garden, he was listed as a witness at the trial of Thomas Hardy (*The Trial of Mr. Thomas Hardy . . .* op cit. (note 23)). On the 30 July the Privy Council had given permission for the prisoners in the Tower to 'walk occasionally on the Parade, ramparts etc' but they were forbidden to speak to anyone (PRO PC 2/140).

[110] Miss Johnson may have been either a daughter or sister of Joseph Johnson (1739–1809), Horne Tooke's publisher, member of the SCI, and prominent figure in radical literary circles.

[111] Mrs. Bonney's sister was an Ann Tomkin, who had permission to accompany Mrs. Bonney on visits to her husband (PRO PC 2/140 fo. 189, printed pagination 100), and, later, permission for Mr. Charles Tomkin as well, presumably Ann's husband. In 1798 a Montague Tomkin produced a bust of Horne Tooke.

[112] Presumably the wife of the Mr. J. F. Tuffin, brandy merchant, who was a member of the SCI. But the text could also be read as 'M^r. Duffin'. Patrick William Duffin, in the Fleet Prison in December 1792 with Thomas Lloyd, was a United Irishman who may have been in the Tower at the same time as JHT. Duffin among others later provided JHT with information on conditions in Coldbath-fields prison which Tooke forwarded to Burdett as part of his campaign against the prison authorities (J. Ann Hone, op. cit. (note 4), p. 92). Below, in the entry for 15 August, JHT mentions sending some birds to Mr. Tuffin. But he might have meant Duffin, confusing the two names (It seems unlikely that he would be sending birds to Mr. Tuffin). However, later on in the diary, on 22 August, JHT is receiving '1 dozen of fine madeira and 1 doz. old Hock' this time definitely from Mrs. Tuffin. Mrs. Tuffin kept an establishment in Thames Street, where on 13 September 1792 a meeting was convened to organize the Fund for assisting the French in the Cause of Freedom (PRO TS 11/951/3495 fo. 1), to which Mr. J. F. Tuffin subscribed £50.

[113] Stephens described Horne Tooke's mode of dress as savouring of the old school, and specifically mentioned that 'he wore long ruffles at the wrist' (Alexander Stephens, op. cit. (note 5), II, p. 234).

[114] Not likely to be the Thomas Wardle charged with high treason but not yet apprehended. Trump Street is off Cheapside between King Street and Wood Street. Perhaps 'M^r. Wardell' was a poulterer although he is not listed as such in the London directories.

[115] It would seem that the broad walk in the grounds of the Tower was a popu-

lar rendezvous for sections of the London gentry. See previous and subsequent references to seeing in this way persons (other than those visiting the prisoners) known to Horne Tooke. Although prisoners were forbidden to speak to such visitors (see above, n. 109), the freedom to walk there rather makes a mockery of the stringent security previously ordered by the Privy Council for the prisoners. Eventually, even the no-talking rule was modified to allow polite exchanges provided a warder were present.

William Styles was a commissioner for customs for England and Wales from 1788 to 1799.

[116] Erasmus Darwin, op. cit. (note 102). The reference to Horne Tooke is as follows:

Whence it appears [in *The Diversions of Purley*], that all languages consist only of nouns and verbs, with their abbreviations for the greater expedition of communicating our thoughts; as explained in the ingenious work of Mr Horne Tooke, who has unfolded by a single flash of light the whole theory of language, which had so long lain buried beneath the learned schools.

II, p. 531 (section XXXIX. 8. 3)

[117] Dr. William Vincent (1739–1815), headmaster of Westminster School. His *The Origination of the Greek Verb: an hypothesis* was published in 1794. On pp. 6–7 of this work he paid tribute to Horne Tooke's *The Diversions of Purley* as seminal to his own ideas.

[118] Thomas Beddoes (1760–1808), physician.

[119] Dr. Pearson's articles in *Transactions of the Royal Society* are: vol. 81 (1791) 'Experiments and observations to investigate the composition of James's powders'; vol. 88 (1798) 'Experiments and observations tending to show the composition and properties of urinary concretions'. It was presumably the latter which Dr. Pearson wished to discuss with Horne Tooke.

[120] Robert Watt and David Downie were committed in May 1794 for high treason in Edinburgh. A special commission was issued in September. Watt was tried and convicted on 3 September and hanged just before the commencement of the trials in London. Downie, although convicted, was recommended to mercy and conditionally pardoned. Watt had previously been on Dundas's payroll as a spy (See Henry W. Meikle, op. cit. (note 99), pp. 89–90). It would seem that he was extraordinarily inept and was possibly double-crossed by his employer. This was the view of *The New Annual Register, or General Repository of History, Politics, and Literature, for the Year 1794* (London, 1795), 'British and Foreign History for the Year 1794', pp. 267–68.

[121] The London Militia Act, 34 Geo. III c. 81 of 7 July 1794, amended acts of 13 and 14 Charles II. It was introduced to reconstitute the City of London Militia by a ballot of ratepayers. *The Times* acknowledged four principal objections. First, that 'previous to this Bill the City had the sole direction of its own Military'. Second, that the bill had been hurried through the Court of Common Council and the House of Commons. Third, that it was oppressive.

Fourth, that the bill was 'the mere vehicle of emolument to the Field Officers' (25 September 1794, p. 4a).

The Militia Act was popularly associated with the crimping issue, which blew up at the same time (See J. Stevenson, 'The London "crimp" riots of 1794', *International Review of Social History*, 16 (1971), 40–58, from which is taken most of the following note).

[122] The nights of 20 and 21 August were the worst nights of the rioting which had begun on 15 August when the body of a young man named George Howe was found, with hands tied behind his back, outside a notorious London crimping house. He had apparently being trying to escape and had fallen from the roof. The justice who happened to be on the spot was Sheridan, who made much of the incident and ordered searches of adjoining houses. Rumours of kidnapping and other atrocities were rife before this, however. Crimps were agents who exploited the unwary or the vulnerable for the bounty paid by the government for new army recruits and whose modes of operation were notoriously corrupt and often criminal.

The riots were considered to have been the most serious London had seen since the Gordon riots of 1780. Because of difficulties of identification and a perceived need to bring charges that juries would find difficult to dismiss, only twenty-three people were eventually committed for trial, of whom four were sentenced to death. The authorities were quick to attempt to establish links between the riots and the societies which they perceived as seditious. Patrick Colquhoun, magistrate at the Worship Street office, was particularly adamant on this point. He believed the riots were 'the result of a deliberate system originating with the corresponding societies for the purposes of introducing anarchy and confusion into the capital that they may with more ease carry into execution these designs which they are hatching for the purpose of overthrowing the government' (Colquhoun to King, 22 August 1794, PRO HO 42/33, quoted in J. Stevenson, op. cit. (note 121), 51). See also *The Times* of 23 August 1794, p. 2b, which indirectly accused the societies of leading on the rioters, who, it noted, frequently cried out '*Liberty, Fraternity, and* PEACE WITH FRANCE'. Beyond a few handbills, hard evidence of such activity by the societies was, however, scant.

[123] I.e. John Wilkes; hence Horne Tooke's implied surprise cum satisfaction, although he should not have been all that surprised that Wilkes should still think kindly of him. Wilkes had, after all, supported him in his election bid against Fox for Westminster in 1790. See Biographical Index.

[124] Horne Tooke may be referring here to the City Horse Volunteers, mentioned in *The Times* reports on the riots (23 August 1794, p. 2b) as having been 'out on duty every day'. Consisting mainly of the upper classes such volunteer bodies were notoriously unpopular with the mass of the people.

[125] See n. 83 for previous mention of the Dundas family in this connection. Charles Dundas (1751–1832) was a member of a different branch of the family. He was returned MP for Berkshire on 16 September 1794.

George Rose (1744–1818), an assiduous promoter of his family's interest within government circles, had worked with Horne Tooke during the Westminster election of 1788, when Lord Hood had been the government candidate. JHT nevertheless seems to view the younger Rose's election in a sinister light: George Rose (1770–1855) was returned for Southampton in a by-election on 26 August 1794.

'Alien Bill' refers to the bill enacted as 33 Geo. III c. 4 (1792) to expel unwanted foreigners. Treyer, who was Horne Tooke's snuff merchant, was spared expulsion unlike the less fortunate Count Zenobio. See n. 22.

[126] Perhaps this was largely true, although Stephens stated (long after the event of course) that the prisoners had communicated quite easily simply by hanging out of their windows when no one was passing (Alexander Stephens, op. cit. (note 5), II, p. 122). This seems very possible especially in regard to Kyd, who was housed directly below Horne Tooke. It is difficult to see how else JHT might have got hold of the Kyd letter to the Privy Council transcribed by JHT on 29 July except by the same method by which JHT lowered the bottle of wine to Kyd's warder (diary entry, 13 June) and presumably retrieved it. See also JHT's marginal note 'I learn from M[r.] Kyd . . . ' (*c.* 15 August in bottom margin of p. 139 of *DoP*). Of course JHT may have been indulging here in one of his characteristic legal pedantries. He may not have actually 'spoken' but communicated by note passed from window to window, although of course he did actually offer greetings to Mrs. Kyd (15 August) and mentions (*c.* 15 August in top margin of p. 139 of *DoP*) that 'M[rs.] Martin says . . . '. Bonney may have been JHT's neighbour on the same floor. Mrs. Thelwall, *The Life of John Thelwall. By his widow*, vol. I (London, 1837; no more published), p. 192, and [J. Thelwall], *The Tribune. . . . Consisting chiefly of the political lectures of J. Thelwall, taken in shorthand by W. Ramsay, and revised by the lecturer*, 3 vols. (London, 1795, 1796), III, p. 238, suggest that conversations between the prisoners were, towards the end of their period in the Tower, quite frequent.

[127] Lydia Hardy died, it is generally accepted, as the result of a miscarriage following injuries she received in an attack on Hardy's house in Piccadilly by a mob celebrating Admiral Howe's 'Glorious First of June' victory over the French. The level of personal invective directed at the reformers by elements of the press may be gauged by the following report of Mrs. Hardy's death by the government-subsidized *St. James's Chronicle* (28–30 August, p. 4c):

Wednesday night died universally lamented, by the insidious Republicans of this city *Mistress* HARDY, wife of *Secretary* HARDY the Cobler, now in confinement for High Treason. — It is supposed the Lady's nerves were so affected by frightful dreams of the hanging, drawing and quartering of her dear *Tommy*, as to have produced the disorder which bro't on her untimely end; a catastrophe to be bewailed by every lover of pure Democracy and Mob Government, and a convincing proof of the inhumanity of Ministry towards the *Fair Sex*.

Note the complete absence of any mention of the mob attack on the Hardy house. In the same celebration the homes of Wilkes and of Lord Stanhope were also wrecked.

[128] This otherwise incomprehensible remark may be Horne Tooke simply recording yet another instance of official corruption, i.e., Tower officers engaging in deals to acquire surplus military equipment. In the same way he has already noted the Cornwallis hangers-on employed in the Tower.

[129] References to a John Pearson occur in a list of names headed 'Compositions layed before me' on 100/01/v and there is another in the list of names on 102/03/r (J. Pearson. See n. 3). This was probably the law student and member of the SCI who was interviewed by the Privy Council and who appears in the indictment as a co-conspirator having been bailed on account of his poor health. Joseph Farington in his diary for Monday 22 December 1794 records the report of his surgeon Robert Batty (who had dined at Horne Tooke's house in Wimbledon the previous day) that 'Kidd, the Counsellor, & Pearson, a young Counsellor, also dined at Tookes. Batty thinks the latter an inflammatory young man' (Joseph Farington, *The Diary of Joseph Farington*, ed. Kenneth Garlick and Angus Macintyre, 16 vols. (New Haven and London, 1978–84), I (1978), p. 280).

However it seems doubtful that the Privy Council would have allowed *this* John Pearson to visit JHT (although see n. 140). It is more likely to have been the London-based Yorkshire surgeon, John Pearson (1758–1826), who about this time was surgeon to the public dispensary in Carey Street. See *DNB* and [Peter Barfoot and John Wilkes (compilers)], op. cit. (note 58), p. 462. This was an institution patronized by the legal profession. Among its vice-presidents were Serjeant Adair and John Silvester, respectively common serjeant and counsel of the Lord Mayor's Court.

The Dr. Vincent mentioned could be the dean of Westminster and author of *The Origination of the Greek Verb: an hypothesis* (London, 1794); but again, in this context, may be a doctor of medicine.

[130] Horne Tooke in writing through Cline in this superficially formal manner seems to be engaging in some kind of verbal nonsense. It is apparent from the content of the letter that the recipient is far from being a stranger. See n. 132.

[131] See note 64 to 'Introduction'.

[132] This slightly bizarre letter was written to the Irishman John Macnamara (1756–1818) (see Biographical Index). Macnamara had been travelling on the continent for the previous three years and had only returned to England in July 1794. Evidently he had left some of his personal belongings with Horne Tooke. During the trial of Thomas Hardy it was suggested that Macnamara had attempted to intimidate one of the prosecution witnesses, the spy Edward Gosling, at the London Coffee House ('The Trial of Thomas Hardy for High Treason', in T. B. and T. J. Howell (compilers), op. cit. (note 5), XXIV (34 & 35 George III . . . A.D. 1794) (London, 1818), col. 730). He subsequently appeared on JHT's behalf at his trial.

Another copy of this letter in JHT's handwriting, obviously not intended for postage, and with Cline's name scratched out, is with other miscellaneous items in the British Library (C. 60. m. 6): John Horne Tooke, [A collection of pamphlets and single sheets . . .] [1778–1812], II.

Other references to Macnamara in the diary occur in financial calculations: *The Diversions of Purley*, p. 140 (not included here), and at 180/81/v.

[133] [Peter Barfoot and John Wilkes (compilers)], op. cit. (note 58), p. 27, lists Lloyd Hill Esq., major of the Tower, at 182*l*.10*s*. per annum. But the army list for 1794 (op. cit. (note 95)) lists Matthew Smith.

[134] The army list for 1795 (op. cit. (note 18)) gives William Windham Dalling as lieutenant and captain of the 3rd regiment of Foot Guards. Possessor of a good Norfolk name, he was possibly a godson of William Windham, the coiner of the phrase (which so irked Horne Tooke) 'convicted felons' to describe Horne Tooke and the others of the twelve charged but acquitted in 1794.

[135] Presumably 'lash' = whip, as in 'whip hand'. By the 'old Laws and constitution' Horne Tooke presumably means the established laws which he and his fellow reformers always claimed the government was seeking to subvert.

[136] This is almost certainly Joseph Gurney the famous shorthand expert who published many of the trials of the period, including JHT's. Ramsey was also a shorthand writer. He recorded John Frost's trial in 1793 (T. B. and T. J. Howell (compilers), op. cit. (note 5), XXII (23–34 George III . . . A.D. 1783–1794) (London, 1817), cols. 471 ff.).

[137] There were two Captain Morrises who wrote convivial songs at this time, the brothers Charles Morris (1745–1838) and Thomas Morris (1732–post-1806) (See *DNB*, and also S. Austin Allibone, *A Critical Dictionary of English Literature and British and American Authors* (Philadelphia, 1870)). However the best known was the avid Foxite Whig and member of the Beefsteak Club, Captain Charles Morris. He published a 'New Song . . . Addressed to John Bull and his numerous Family' about this time (British Library gives the date of publication as 1795), in which he attacked the ministry for leading England into the war with France. It comprised twenty-five four-line stanzas, too long to quote here in full; but stanzas 9, 21, and 22 give some idea of why it appealed to Horne Tooke:

> But to set out a tilting, and shake your weak lance
> Against millions of men, arm'd for *freedom*, in France,
> Was a twist in your head, Master BULL, d'ye see —
> Mighty strange *in your nation, that made itself free.*
>
> Big curses by day, ay bigger by night
> On the JENKY-nurs'd Jackall, that brought on this plight!
> Who has *stalk'd in Court stilts* to that ruinous brink,
> Where 'tis hopeless to move — and more hopeless to think.

A while your brave *tars*, the great *prop of your state*
Have, by glory and conquest, JOHN, put off your fate;
But if e'er on French *decks* shouts of *victory roar*,
The Crown's a Red Night Cap, and Britain's *no more*.

'JENKY' is presumably Charles Jenkinson, Baron Hawkesbury (later 1st earl of Liverpool), president of the Board of Trade: Pitt is the 'JENKY-nurs'd Jackall'.

[138] For the function of the special commission of oyer and terminer see n. 108. The commissioners, apart from the president of the court, Sir James Eyre, lord chief justice of the Common Pleas, were: the marquis of Tichfield, Sir Beaumont Hotham; Sir N. Grose; Sir Charles Morgan; John Silvester; William Mainwaring; Paul Joddrell; John Lewis; John Pownall; Rt. Hon. H. Hobart; Sir Archibald McDonald; Sir Francis Buller; Sir Soulden Lawrence; Sir J. W. Rose; Cranley Tho. Kirby; Edward Montague; Samuel Wegg; Anthony Dickens; and Henry Barlow (*The Trial of Mr. Thomas Hardy . . .* op. cit. (note 23), p. 9). There was also a grand jury of either twenty-one or twenty-three men. The numbers and names vary according to the source. *The Trial of Mr. Thomas Hardy . . .* op. cit. (note 23), p. 10, records twenty-three; 'The Trial of Thomas Hardy for High Treason', in T. B. and T. J. Howell (compilers), op. cit. (note 5), XXIV (34 & 35 George III . . . A.D. 1794) (London, 1818), col. 200, records twenty-one.

[139] This may be James Perry (1756–1821), member of the Friends of the People, editor and proprietor of the *Morning Chronicle*, who had himself been prosecuted in 1793 for seditious libel and may have harboured a fellow feeling towards Horne Tooke. Other references mention 'Mʳ. Perry of Oxford Street' sending JHT a 'Pye' (27 August) and JHT's seeing 'Perry paſs by' (11 October), presumably on the walks in the Tower. However JHT had connections with at least four different Perrys: 'Mʳ. Perry of Oxford Street', 'Mr Perry — pastrycook', Capt. Perry, and one unspecified other. See the 1792 Fund for assisting the French (PRO TS 11/951/3495 fo. 19), and JHT's list of those persons to whom he sent his 'blue-bound' copies of *Proceedings in an Action for Debt . . .* (London, 1792) in 1792 (flyleaf notes in copy bound in British Library (C. 60. m. 6), John Horne Tooke [A collection of pamphlets and single sheets . . .] [1778–1812], II). On 31 December 1793 a William Perry, surgeon of H.M.S. *Assistance*, wrote to Nepean to inform upon 'an unfortunate relation of mine now in France' who had apparently conducted 'treacherous correspondence from King's Bench prison' — whether one of JHT's Perrys is not known (PRO TS 11/957/3502).

[140] G.J.W. in his 1897 *Notes & Queries* extracts from the diary makes this passage read: 'Tom Symonds tells me Mr Joyce's brother (told him) that a friend of his, who dined with Mr Pitt . . . ' (G.J.W., 'Horne Tooke's Diary', *Notes and Queries*, Eighth Series 11 (January–June 1897), no. 263 (9 January 1897), 21–22). It would be more plausible, however, that JHT meant to write either 'Tom Symonds (Mr. Joyce's brother) tells me that a friend of his . . .' or 'Tom

Symonds tells me that Mr. Joyce's brother, a friend of his, . . .'. Thomas Symonds, of Crown-office Row, Inner Temple, student at law and member of the SCI, was subpoenaed as a prosecution witness. According to the evidence before the Privy Council of Christopher Hull (an exceedingly garrulous witness), Symonds always disagreed with Horne Tooke at SCI meetings (PRO PC 2/140 fo. 275, printed pagination 140). But exactly how Symonds told Horne Tooke about this event is not explained.

Indeed at this stage security at the Tower seems to have all but broken down with regard to visitors. There is no record in the Privy Council Register, for example, of the earlier visits on 6 September of Dr. Vincent and of John Pearson; or of the visit of Captain Chivers (or Shivers) on 5 October. There is certainly none for Symonds. Note, however, that on 1 October 'F —— ' was prevented from seeing Horne Tooke by the warder Bateman. Perhaps by this stage it had become rather arbitrary — undermined by continuing Privy Council concessions and by Yorke's seeming capitulation to Horne Tooke's demands of 24 August.

[141] The so-called Pop-gun Plot. On 27 September Paul Thomas Lemaitre, apprentice to a watch-case maker, William Higgins, apprentice to a chemist, and the bookseller John Smith, all members of the LCS, were apprehended by a warrant from the home secretary, the duke of Portland, and examined on the 28th before the Privy Council. According to the testimony of an informer, Thomas John Upton, a watchmaker, also a member of the LCS, the plan involved the construction of a walking-stick with a brass tube inserted which would have permitted a poisoned arrow or dart to be blown by Lemaitre at the king, either on the terrace at Windsor or in the play-house. Instantaneous death was meant to have been the result. *The New Annual Register* (op. cit. at note 120), 'British and Foreign History for the Year 1794', p. 269, considered that 'a more ridiculous, inconsistent and improbable tale never was invented', and suggested a party-political motive; see also *Assassination of the King! The Conspirators exposed, or an account of the apprehension, treatment in prison and repeated examinations Before the Privy Council of John Smith and George Higgins on a charge of High Treason* (London, printed for John Smith at the Pop-Gun, Portsmouth Street, Lincoln's Inn Fields, 1795). The suspects were eventually released the following year without charge.

[142] The first of these 'execrable schemes' was probably the Pop-gun Plot: see preceding note. The second may have been the suspected rigging of the juries for the forthcoming trials. William Godwin remarked:

Reports have been propagated of a very extraordinary nature, respecting the manner of forming a Jury. These reports, if not legally proved, have never been contradicted; and therefore ought to be stated, that, if false, they may be contradicted. It is said, that the Sheriffs, instead of suffering the Jury to be struck, at the place where the book of the Freeholders is kept, and by the Officers to whom that care ordinarily falls, sent for the books from the office, and took the task upon themselves. It is farther affirmed, that, in consequence, various mistakes were made; and some persons were summoned upon the

Grand Jury, and the Petty Jury; and letters of summons sent to the one, that ought to have been sent to the other. . . . It is obvious to every person that casts his eye over the list, that it consists of a most extraordinary assemblage, King's tradesmen, contractors, and persons labouring under every kind of bias and influence; very few indeed that can at all pretend to independence and impartiality; and perhaps those few to be ultimately challenged by the Officers of the Crown. Thus every part of the transaction appears to be uniform, and marks an administration, callous to public character, and determined to employ all means indiscriminately to effect their sanguinary purpose.

> [William Godwin], *Cursory Strictures on the Charge delivered by Lord Chief Justice Eyre to the Grand Jury, October 2, 1794* (London, 1794), Appendix II, pp. 51–52 (originally published in the *Morning Chronicle* for 24 October 1794).

[143] Conceivably this could be John Frost, Francis Vaughan, or the warder Finney. As noted earlier (n. 140), security may have slackened in regard to the prisoners' visitors; if so, the 'F——' was most likely to have been someone perhaps of junior or equal status to Bateman, and unlikely to complain to higher authority, e.g. the warder Finney.

[144] Messrs. George and Romaine William Clarkson of Essex Street were Horne Tooke's solicitors (T. B. and T. J. Howell (compilers), op. cit. (note 5), XXV (35 & 36 George III . . . A.D. 1794–1796) (London, 1818), col. 5).

[145] The first three volumes of the Revd. Christopher Wyvill (1740–1822), *Political Papers chiefly respecting the attempt of the County of York and other . . . districts commenced in 1779 . . . to effect a reformation of the Parliament of Great Britain*, 6 vols. (York, 1794–1802), were published in 1794. In this form they were cited in the catalogue of Horne Tooke's library, auctioned after his death ([John Horne Tooke], op. cit. (note 89), item 801). Volume 4 did not appear till 1796. Wyvill, a moderate in his reform programme, and in the 1780s an antagonist of the Jebb/Cartwright-led SCI, appeared for Horne Tooke at his trial.

[146] Probably the *British Synonymy; . . .* , 2 vols. (London, 1794) of Hester Lynch Thrale, afterwards Piozzi (1741–1821), which is listed in the catalogue of JHT's library auctioned after his death ([John Horne Tooke], op. cit. (note 89), item 540).

[147] John Money, *The History of the Campaign of 1792, between the Armies of France and the Allies . . .* (London, 1794). Auctioned as part of Horne Tooke's library ([John Horne Tooke], op. cit. (note 89), item 477).

[148] The king's speeches to parliament were published, immediately after delivery, by Charles Eyre & Andrew Strahan, as folio pamphlets of four pages. Horne Tooke is probably referring to a collection of such speeches bound up as a volume.

[149] These papers may have carried reports of the SCI meeting at the Crown and Anchor of that date, at which Horne Tooke defended the British constitution. See JHT's entry for 5 August and n. 105.

[150] These were probably the reports of the Committees of Secrecy of the House of Commons and of the House of Lords. Members of the special commission and of the grand jury of 2 October 1794 were all given copies of the reports. See Sir James Eyre's opening speech to the commission (*The Trial of Mr. Thomas Hardy . . .* op. cit. (note 23), p. 11).

[151] The form by which a grand jury sends, or does not send, a case for trial; see n. 108. If no bill is found against those charged, the case against them fails and no further trial is necessary. At this stage it is hard to guess whether JHT would have welcomed such a scenario.

[152] Eyre's charge was delivered to the grand jury of the special commission on 2 October 1794 at the session house on Clerkenwell Green: 'That which hath given occasion for this Commission is that which is declared by a late statute [the Suspension of Habeas Corpus], namely, "that a traitorous and detestable conspiracy has been formed for subverting the existing laws and constitution, and for introducing the system of anarchy and confusion which has so lately prevailed in France" '. There were nine specific charges based on 25 Edward III (1350).

[153] This somewhat mysterious reference suggests once again that security was not as tight as previously (see n. 140). No Captain Chivers is identifiable from the army list (opera citata (notes 18 and 95)). Perhaps it was Thomas Revell Shivers, captain, RN.

[154] Either an anonymous handbill denouncing the trials which Campbell had found or been given, or else a private letter which he thought contained relevant information.

[155] Presumably a notice accompanying the Order for Trial signed by members of the Privy Council on 7 October (PRO PC 2/141).

[156] I.e. that the grand jury had found true bills against the prisoners. They were found against all except John Lovett.

[157] According to Erskine's opening address to the court he had at first intended to conduct his defence of Horne Tooke with the aim simply of securing his individual acquittal, but JHT had rejected this strategy: 'he has charged me', Erskine claimed, 'to waste and destroy my strength to prove that no such guilt can be brought home to others' (Alexander Stephens, op. cit. (note 5), II, p. 146). How much of this was simply courtroom histrionics we have no way of telling. But this comment of JHT's might be referring to this address.

When JHT had this interview with Erskine, Gibbs, and Clarkson, it was in the very early stages of defence preparation. It was still sixteen days to the arraignment on 25 October and it is quite possible that JHT, the most experienced and arguably the most intellectually able of those indicted, did influence the overall defence strategy.

But in any case JHT did take a very active part in his own trial, conducting his own cross-examination of witnesses and from the very start complaining about his counsel's strategy with regard to the prosecution's jury challenges. Erskine would have been well aware of his client's court-room abilities. Horne

Tooke had, as he said to Lord Chief Justice Eyre at his trial, 'been forty years a student' of the law (a reference to his having been refused admittance to the bar because he was in holy orders). The legal expertise of his co-defendants was less obvious. When Thelwall announced that he would be hanged if he did not defend himself, Erskine assured him that he would be hanged if he did.

[158] Because of possible challenges to jurors by defence as well as prosecution lawyers it was necessary to have many more jurors than would eventually be called to form the twelve-man jury. The 207 witnesses were presumably all prosecution witnesses, all of whom would have to be closely studied by the defence team in the limited time available. By Horne Tooke's assessment (435 divided by 10) his team would have to scrutinize at least 43½ jurors/witnesses per day in order to get through them all. Perhaps Horne Tooke is also making the point that the elaborate scale of the preparations demonstrated the fact that the trial, as far as he was concerned, was rigged.

[159] By this Horne Tooke probably meant that he had recognized most of the others as being members of Reeves's loyal associations. However, the ultimate verdict on the juries of *The New Annual Register* (op. cit. at note 120), 'British and Foreign History for the Year 1794', p. 271, was:

Whatever calumnies may have been unjustly cast upon the loyal associations in the beginning of 1793, it is a sufficient refutation of them to say, that most of the gentlemen who composed this and the other juries were members of these associations. Perhaps, indeed, a more respectable, impartial, intelligent and attentive jury never was impanelled, than that which sat upon the present occasion.

[160] At this point Horne Tooke has recorded almost nothing in his diary for nine days save for the visits of Cline. He may have been working on his defence. Doubtless he needed to prepare his opening speech and to plan, as far as possible, court-room strategies. But the gap seems to indicate deepening depression and fatalism rather than feverish activity. At this stage he was probably convinced of his own observation of 26 September that the state meant to perpetrate a 'long-prepared murder'.

[161] Presumably Richard Sharp (1759–1835), MP, hatter, host, and critic, friend of the Hollands. Byron referred to him in 1813 as 'a man of elegant mind and who has lived much with the best — Fox, Horne Tooke, Windham, Fitzpatrick, and all the agitators of other times and tongues' (quoted in R.G. Thorne (ed.), op. cit. (note 33), v, p. 130).

[162] They were taken in hackney coaches guarded by constables but no military. When Horne Tooke arrived at Newgate 'the Jailor [John Kirby] refused to admit him, as no warrant could be produced for his commitment. His nephew, therefore, returned to the Tower to secure the necessary papers, while his uncle sat in a comfortable room before a blazing fire' (Alexander Stephens op. cit. (note 5), II, p. 124).

[163] See Horne Tooke's entry for Thursday 23 October, in which he indicates that Erskine and Gibbs were to visit him at 3.30 p.m. the following day. At his

arraignment on the 25th JHT made much of his sudden removal to Newgate and consequent loss of his opportunity to consult his counsel:

My Lord, in a great measure am I prevented from being able to say any thing on the subject of the indictment, for the circumstance of our not having had the ten clear days allowed by Act of Parliament, to persons in our situation. By the change of custody a whole day has been completely lost to us; in consequence, we have not had an opportunity of conversing with our Counsel. Mr *Erskine* and Mr *Gibbs* had engaged themselves to dine with me on Friday, for the purposes of conferring together in the business of this day. Notice was given me as late as nine or ten on Thursday night only of my intended removal; I was removed by eight o'clock the next morning; it was perfectly impossible for me, therefore, to take the advantage of my Counsel's advice, as our arrangements were completely destroyed, and all my papers, which I had collected and arranged in the Tower, thrown into disorder and confusion . . .

The Trial of Mr. Thomas Hardy . . . op. cit. (note 23), pp. 49–50.

BIOGRAPHICAL INDEX

This index lists only the more significant persons named in Introduction, Text of Diary, and Notes, and selects only the more important references. Numerals refer to pages; superscript numerals identify notes.

BAXTER, John (no dates available). A member of the LCS and delegate to the joint LCS/SCI Committee of Secrecy (or Correspondence). One of the twelve indicted with Horne Tooke for high treason. According to the court (see *The Trial of Mr. Thomas Hardy for High Treason: containing the whole of the proceedings . . . and the bills of indictment found against Thomas Hardy, John Horne Tooke, John Augustus Bonney* [and others] . . . *Accurately taken in short-hand by Manoah Sibley* (Dublin, 1794), p. 49) he was a labourer but is referred to in Stephens as an engraver (Alexander Stephens, *Memoirs of J. Horne Tooke*, 2 vols. (London, 1813) II, p. 301) and as a silversmith by Brown (Philip A. Brown, *The French Revolution in English History* (London, 1918), p. 119). Initially, the crown does not appear to have been very interested in him. He was not interviewed by the Privy Council till 7 July although implicated by the evidence (21 May) of the bookseller, John Hillier, in the nebulous Parrot public-house scenario (pikes and drilling) and was said to 'lead a good deal as he can speak well'. He was eventually incarcerated in Newgate. — 9, 10, 17

BONNEY, John Augustus (1763–1813). Attorney and member of the SCI. An active campaigner for the radical cause, he assisted in the defence of Thomas Paine, Daniel Isaac Eaton, John Binns, Arthur O'Connor, and Thomas Thompson. He was attorney to Horne Tooke in Fox's action for debt in April 1792. With John Frost, to whom he had been articled, he was a legal adviser to Sir Francis Burdett during his successful election campaign for Middlesex in 1802.

From an entry by Farington in his diary (27 June 1794) it would seem that at the time of his arrest Bonney held a position with the Commissioners for Paving. Bonney's wife importuned Farington to assist in obtaining the position for Thomas Hague (her brother) till Bonney's trial was over. This seems to have been accomplished (Joseph Farington, *The Diary of Joseph Farington*, ed. Kenneth Garlick and Angus Macintyre, 16 vols. (New Haven and London, 1978–84), I (1978), p. 205).

Bonney's sketchy diary of his arrest and imprisonment is printed in Nicholas Roe, *The Politics of Nature: Wordsworth and some contemporaries* (Basingstoke, 1992), pp. 85–97. — 9, 10, 17, 39, 43, 50, 53, 54, 61, 62, 67, 72, 91[48]

CARTWRIGHT, Major John (1740–1824). Country gentleman and reformer; founder, with Dr. John Jebb, of the SCI. A close associate of JHT although not sharing his reservations about universal suffrage. Brother of the inventor of the power loom, the Revd. Edmund Cartwright, and himself somewhat addicted to mechanical thinking. — 3, 6, 18, 20, 61, 80[1], 102[106]

CLINE, Henry (1750–1827). Surgeon at St. Thomas's Hospital. Cline was a devoted follower of Horne Tooke and a friend of John Thelwall. It was at Cline's house that Horne Tooke and some of his supporters celebrated immediately after his acquittal. — 44, 49, 50, 51, 52, 53, 54, 55, 56, 57, 58, 59, 60, 61, 62, 63, 64, 65, 66, 67, 68–70, 71, 72, 73, 74, 75, 76, 77, 78, 93[58], 96[77]

DUNDAS, Henry (1742–1811). Till July 1794 secretary of state in the Home Department; after July 1794 secretary of state for war. He was a neighbour of JHT's at Wimbledon, a fact which particularly galled JHT (See JHT's diary entry for 14 July and Alexander Stephens, op. cit. (s. n. Baxter), II, pp. 160, 188). With strong political and family links in Scotland he was perceived by many as Scotland's uncrowned king. His nephew, Robert Dundas, was lord advocate of Scotland, and through him Dundas was closely involved in the prosecution of the Scottish reformers in 1793–94. — 2, 10, 14, 33, 35, 44, 48, 53, 55, 83[10], 92[55], 99[91], 101[99]

ERSKINE, Hon. Thomas (1750–1823). Barrister; MP for Portsmouth. He was the most successful barrister and, in 1806–07, the least distinguished lord chancellor of his day. In the law courts he was active in defence of progressive causes. In the House of Commons he was a leader of the prince of Wales's faction. — 17, 76, 77, 78, 98[88], 112[157], 113[163]

EYRE, Sir James (1734–99). Lord chief justice of the common pleas from February 1793, a member of the Privy Council, and presiding judge at the trials of Hardy, Horne Tooke, and Thelwall. — 12, 14, 15, 16, 25[31], 72

FAWKENER, William (?–1811). Secretary to the Privy Council and to the Board of Trade. — 33, 44, 46, 49, 61, 86[15], 87[23]

FORD, Richard (1758–1806). Magistrate; MP, April 1789–May 1791. Magistrate at Shadwell police office (1792), and at Bow Street (1794). Employed by the Home Office to collect information on the societies. Knighted in 1801, Ford later became chief magistrate at the Bow Street office (1800). — 33, 35, 36, 86[15], 87[23]

FROST, John (?1750–1842). Gentleman attorney; an early member of the SCI and close associate of Horne Tooke. Once an ally of Pitt in his reform period, he became a *bête noire* of the establishment. With the American writer and politician, Joel Barlow, he presented the address of the SCI to the national convention of France in 1792 and was present at the passing of the death sentence upon Louis XVI, a circumstance duly noted by Edmund Burke. In 1793, on a trumped-up charge of uttering, when drunk, 'seditious words', i.e. 'equality and no king', he was described (in the indictment) as 'a person of a depraved, impious, and disquiet mind, and of a seditious disposition', was sentenced to six months in Newgate and an hour in the pillory at Charing Cross, and was required to find sureties for his good behaviour for five years; a sentence which Lord Campbell two generations later described as excessive, and unfitting for a gentleman. Lord Kenyon also ordered that he be struck off the roll of attorneys, 'whereby he was to be rendered infamous and to be irretrievably ruined' (John Campbell, Baron Campbell, *The Lives of the Chief Justices of England*, 3 vols. (London, 1849, 1857), III (1857), p. 50). He escaped his period in the pillory thanks to a near-riot on his behalf. Horne Tooke on that occasion walked him through the crowds back into custody (obituary notice 12 July 1842: British Library, Additional MS 27817 fo. 154). He was called as a witness in the trial of Thomas Hardy and was described in 1794 as 'late of Spring-garden, Westminster, but now of Pinner, gentleman, late attorney of the court of the King's Bench' (*The Trial of Mr. Thomas Hardy . . .* op. cit. (s. n. Baxter)). It is probable that it was only his five-year bond (with sureties) that saved him from arrest and trial. As it was, he was interviewed by the Privy Council on suspicion of treasonable practices (31 May) but was ultimately discharged, having, he said, taken no part in the affairs of the SCI since his release from prison. He later worked with the Horne Tooke/Burdett faction but eventually fell out with them, dying in almost total obscurity at the age of ninety-two. — 4, 5, 10, 40, 56, 89[30], 100[94]

GIBBS, Vicary (1751–1820). Barrister. Counsel with Erskine in the 1794 trials, at which he is said to have first distinguished himself. Attorney general 1807–12. Entered parliament in 1804; knighted in 1805. — 17, 35, 37, 76, 77, 78, 88[26], 112[157], 113[163]

GRENVILLE, William Wyndham Grenville, first baron (1759–1834). Secretary of state in the Foreign Department, ministerial leader in the House of Lords. Pitt's cousin. — 33, 48, 51, 86[16], 95[68], 99[91]

HARDY, Thomas (1752–1832). Shoemaker, founder and secretary of the LCS. Indicted for high treason, 1794. His shoemaking shop prospered in the wake of his trial, though the latter signalled the end of his career as a working-class radical. — 8, 9, 10, 12, 13, 17, 18, 20, 21, 36, 53, 54, 67, 82[9]

HODGSON, Richard (no dates available). Hatter; member of the LCS; member of the joint LCS/SCI Committee of Secrecy (or Correspondence); one of the twelve indicted for high treason in 1794; but he evaded detention. — 9, 10, 17

HOLCROFT, Thomas (1745–1809). Singer, playwright, translator, novelist, friend of William Godwin. Member of the SCI; member of the joint LCS/SCI Committee of Secrecy (or Correspondence); one of the twelve indicted for high treason in 1794, although not detained until after the opening of the trial when he created something of a sensation by voluntarily surrendering himself: 'A premeditated act of gallantry', according to Stephens, 'which produced a great and salutary effect' (Alexander Stephens, op. cit. (s. n. Baxter), II, p. 140). 'Holcroft', declared Farington, 'is avowedly a man of the most loose principles with regard to religion' (Joseph Farington, op. cit. (s. n. Bonney), I (1978), p. 259 (entry for 14 November 1794)). Like Godwin, he believed in the invincible and inevitable power of objective facts over all human affairs. In politics he advocated non-violence. — 5, 6, 9, 10, 16–17

HORNE TOOKE, John (1736–1812). Reformer and philologist; effectively the leader of the SCI from 1792. Tried for high treason in 1794. See 'Introduction' for details of his life. — early life 18–19, 31; later life 21, 22, 27[65]; family 21–22, 90[35], 91[40]; philological work 20–21; ideological position 7, 11, 19–22; trial 14–18; and *passim*

JOYCE, the Revd. Jeremiah (1763–1816). Former journeyman-glazier and Unitarian preacher; tutor to Earl Stanhope's sons; member of the SCI; secretary to the combined LCS/SCI Committee of Secrecy (or Correspondence); imprisoned in the Tower and one of the twelve indicted for high treason in 1794. Later, his plain-language textbooks on science and mathematics were to make him almost a household name. — 8, 9, 10, 11, 17, 43, 48, 53, 54, 72, 74, 80[5]

KYD (Kydd), Stuart/Stewart (?–1811). Scottish-born barrister, legal writer, member of the SCI. Admitted to Middle Temple on 15 June 1782 and to the bar on 22 June 1787. Imprisoned in the Tower and one of the twelve indicted for high treason in 1794, he later (1797) powerfully, if unsuccessfully, defended Thomas Williams for publishing Tom Paine's *The Age of Reason* (Part I: 1794; Part II: 1795). He is recalled by Lord Campbell as the barrister who got the better of Lord Kenyon in a prosecution for blasphemy, being 'improperly permitted to ridicule and stigmatize at great length the most sacred truths of the Gospel' (John Campbell, Baron Campbell, op. cit. (s. n. Frost), III (1857), p. 69). — 9, 10, 11, 17, 40, 43, 48, 53, 58, 72, 84[13]

LOVETT (Lovet/Loveit/Lovatt), John (1777–1816). Hairdresser; prominent member of the LCS. Imprisoned in the Tower but not indicted for high treason in 1794. Because of this the *Biographical Dictionary of Modern British Radicals vol. I: 1770–1830* (ed. Joseph O. Baylen and Norbert J. Gossman (Hassocks (Sussex), 1979)) suggests he was a government spy. But he *was* mentioned in the indictment along with William Sharp and John Pearson as a co-conspirator (*The Trial of Mr. Thomas Hardy* . . . op. cit. (s. n. Baxter)) and there is nothing in the official Privy Council record of his interrogation (16 May) which would confirm that he was a spy. All the same it is odd that a bill was not found against him since he was very active in the LCS, being a member of the combined LCS/SCI Committee of Secrecy (or Correspondence) and chairing the meeting at Chalk Farm on 14 April at which it was resolved to press on with the idea of a national convention, whereas Holcroft, against whom a bill *was* found, although also nominally a member of the Committee of Secrecy, was hardly involved at all in the public affairs of the societies, was never arrested or examined, and in any case preached a doctrine of non-violence. Later Lovett emigrated to New York where he prospered — another reason why the *Biographical Dictionary of Modern British Radicals* thinks he may have been a spy. Christina Bewley in her forthcoming biography of John Horne Tooke maintains that Lovett was Thomas Hardy's brother-in-law. — 9, 10, 16, 53, 54

MACNAMARA, John (1756–1818). MP for Leicester in the interest of the duke of Rutland, 1784–90. An old campaigning friend from the 1788 Westminster elections when both Horne Tooke and Macnamara supported the Pittite candidate Admiral Hood. Macnamara was seriously injured by a pro-Fox mob at the time, sustaining a fractured skull, in which condition he wrote to Horne Tooke on 25 June to come to him immediately with Mr. Vaughan to write to his 'poor wife and children' (quoted in full in R. W. Twigge, *The Pedigree of John Macnamara, Esquire* ([London], 1908), p. 67). His wife, Mary, was the only daughter and heir of Arthur Jones; and young John, who, judging from Horne Tooke's avuncular tone, may have been his godson, was their second son. Macnamara's brother, James, ended his naval career (in spite of a manslaughter charge over a duel in which he was supported in court by his friend Lord Nelson) as rear-admiral of the White. John Macnamara appeared as a witness for Horne Tooke at his trial. — 68–69, 107[132]

MARTIN, John (no dates available). Attorney; member of LCS and associate member of the SCI. He was imprisoned in the Tower at the same time as Horne Tooke and the others in 1794 but was charged with high treason on a separate indictment. The crown clearly wished to prove that he had drunk a toast, while in the King's Bench prison for debt, to 'the King's head in a basket', and it interviewed other prisoners and visitors; although they testified to his intemperate language and especially to that of his wife, Hannah, no one would corroborate the story (PRO PC 2/140 and TS 11/957/3502).

Martin was in the King's Bench at the time of the Chalk Farm meeting of the LCS on 14 April, but the crown's determination to get evidence against him probably arose from his inflammatory 'Hessian troops' speech to the LCS of 20 January 1794: 'Will you wait until Barracks are erected in every village and till *subsidised* Hessians and Hanoverians are upon us?' (Gwyn A. Williams, *Artisans and Sans-Culottes* (London, 1968), pp. 77–78).

Horne Tooke possessed two books by John Martin, both on the legal system of Scotland, 1791, 1792: [John Horne Tooke], *Books. A catalogue of the valuable library, late the property of J. Horne Tooke* [London, 1813], items 459, 460. — 8, 37, 53, 54, 77, 84[13], 94[65]

MOORE, Matthew (no dates available). Scottish tailor; member of the LCS; member of joint LCS/SCI Committee of Secrecy (or Correspondence); one of the speakers at the Chalk Farm meeting on 14 April 1794. Indicted for high treason in 1794, he evaded detention. — 9, 10, 17

NEPEAN, Evan (1752–1822). Under-secretary of state for the Home Department until July 1794. From July 1794, under-secretary of state for war. On 29 May 1792 J. Bland Burges wrote privately to Lord Auckland of Nepean:

At a troublesome moment like the present, his arrival is fortunate, for he is a quick, sensible man, who is used to the police department, and who does business in a spirited and steady way. Talents of this sort may probably be necessary in the approaching summer, when every effort will certainly be made to produce confusion.

> William Eden, Baron Auckland, *The Journal and Correspondence of William, Lord Auckland*, ed. G. Hogge, 4 vols. (London, [1860]–62), II, p. 410.

He entered the House of Commons in 1796. — 2, 9, 33, 34, 51

PEARSON, Dr. George (1751–1828). Physician and chemist, physician to St. George's Hospital, elected FRS on 30 June 1791. He was an intimate friend of Horne Tooke and of Sir Francis Burdett, but took no part in politics. — 44, 49, 50, 51, 53, 61, 63, 64, 67, 68, 71, 73, 76

PITT, William (the younger) (1759–1806). Prime minister and chancellor of the exchequer. Pitt had been a committed advocate of parliamentary reform in the 1780s, putting the question of reform before parliament in 1782, 1783, and 1785. He had, along with Fox, Sheridan, Earl Stanhope, and the duke of Richmond, been closely associated with the SCI and in 1782 had been a delegate with Horne Tooke to a reform convention at which Horne Tooke had actively supported Pitt's plan of reform (Alexander Stephens, op. cit. (s. n. Baxter), II, pp. 40, 144). This was made much of by the defence at the 1794 trials (*The Proceedings at Large on the Trial of John Horne Tooke for High Treason taken in short-hand by J. H. Blanchard*, 2 vols. (London, 1795), II, pp. 71–76). — 1, 2, 3, 7, 9, 12, 14, 18, 51, 55, 72–73, 95[68], 96[78], 99[91]

PORTLAND, William Henry Cavendish Bentinck, third duke of Portland (1738–1809). Leader of the Whig group which entered Pitt's ministry in July 1794, replacing Dundas as home secretary. — 2, 59, 99[91], 101[99]

REEVES, John (1752–1829). Barrister and writer on English law (his *A History of the English Law*, 2 vols. (London, 1783, 1784), had a new edition as late as 1869), commissioner of bankrupts, chief justice of Newfoundland 1791–92, and founder, in November 1792, of the Association of Liberty and Property against Republicans and Levellers, the first of the scores (some assess the number at 2,000) of loyalist associations to spring up all over the country. Reeves had drafted the unsuccessful London and Westminster police bill of 1785 and became receiver under the subsequent legislation of 1792, the Middlesex Justices Act. This was a powerful position appointed directly by the crown, and gave virtual control over the financial administration of the eight newly constituted police offices, and hence over the twenty-four newly appointed stipendiary magistrates (See Leon Radzinowicz, *A History of English Criminal Law and its Administration from 1750*, 5 vols. (London, 1956), III, p. 131).

The active presence of Reeves, subpoenaed to the Hardy trial simply as 'barrister-at-law' (*The Trial of Mr. Thomas Hardy . . .* op. cit. (s. n. Baxter),

p. 37) at the Privy Council interrogations, was reported both by Horne Tooke and others (Richter reported that he not only conducted some of the preliminary interrogations but acted as 'secretary' (British Library, Additional MS 27816 fos. 451–71 at p. 14)), and in the press; it is difficult to explain since he held no appropriate official position. Reeves was not a stipendiary magistrate like Ford, nor would his position as receiver, or that of law clerk to the Board of Trade, explain his presence there. It is possible that he was meant to be present simply as a legal expert, to advise the government, which, until Habeas Corpus was officially suspended, was subject to its provisions.

He was of course the embodiment of virulent anti-Jacobinism, as the men being interrogated would have been well aware. Reeves almost certainly had covert backing from the government for the establishment of his association and for its work in propagating the government line on the war and national security. According to Reeves himself, however, Pitt only saw him about three times in relation to the setting-up of the association, out of 'curiosity', and permitted him the use of the post office for sending out their packages, but was otherwise not involved (Reeves to Windham, 1 August 1794, British Library, Additional MS 37874 fo. 33). His presence in any case, as the arch-Jacobin-baiter, probably represented a psychological advantage for the government.

Reeves was himself prosecuted in 1796 for his 1795 pamphlet, *Thoughts on the English Government* (Part I, London, 1795), in which he insisted that it was feasible to do away with both parliament and the aristocracy so long as the monarchy remained the trunk of the political tree. This was formally objected to as a libel on the constitution by Sheridan in the House of Commons and by the earl of Albemarle in the House of Lords. On this prosecution see A. V. Beedell, 'John Reeves's prosecution for a seditious libel, 1795–96: a study in political cynicism', *The Historical Journal*, 36:4 (1993), 799–824. This prosecution did not injure his career. He was appointed to the remunerative job of king's printer in 1800, a post he had been lobbying for since at least 1794; and he became inspector of aliens in 1802. — 2, 3, 6, 14, 24[11], 33, 51, 52, 97[81]

RICHMOND, Charles Lennox, 3rd duke of (1735–1806). Field-marshal, formerly in Pitt's cabinet, strongly in favour of parliamentary reform. It was his plan of universal representation and annual parliaments that was taken up by the LCS as the core of its reform ideology. — 3, 4, 18, 80[1]

RICHTER, John (?–1830). Banker's clerk employed by Sir Robert Herries; son of the artist John Augustus Richter and brother of the artist Henry Richter, who was a friend of William Blake; member of the LCS and associate member of the SCI. Proposed as an SCI delegate to the British Convention in Edinburgh in October 1793 though he did not go (evidence of George Williams before the Privy Council, PRO TS 11/957/3502/1). He was a prominent speaker at the 14 April Chalk Farm meeting of the LCS, reading out the resolution that the LCS intended to call a national convention in London. Imprisoned in the Tower and one of the thirteen prosecuted for high treason in 1794. His manuscript account of his arrest and imprisonment is amongst the Francis Place papers in the British Library, Additional MS 27816 fos 452–71. — 9, 10, 17, 18, 53

SHARP, William (1749–1824). Engraver; member of the SCI; member of the joint LCS/SCI Committee of Secrecy (or Correspondence), possibly as Horne Tooke's personal deputy. Engraved the symbolical ornamentation for John Cartwright's *Declaration of Principles which are deemed incontrovertible* (London, [?1821]) and the frontispiece to JHT's *The Diversions of Purley*. Although not actually charged, he was mentioned in the indictment as a co-conspirator with the accused and was subpoenaed as a witness to the trial of Thomas Hardy. Although clearly identified as a member of the LCS/SCI Committee of Secrecy (or Correspondence), he seems to have been spared standing trial with the others, in exchange for information. He was interrogated intensively by the Privy Council, but does not seem to have provided any damning evidence, a fact which clearly irritated his interlocutors as did his sometimes rather off-hand and droll responses. He was of course a close friend of JHT, living with him at one stage for two years, and spending weeks at a stretch at Wimbledon teaching his daughters engraving (his examination of 9 June: PRO PC 2/140; Alexander Stephens, op. cit. (s. n. Baxter), II, p. 162). — 10, 11, 40, 51, 93[59], 96[78]

SHERIDAN, Richard Brinsley (1751–1816). Playwright; MP for Stafford; a leader of the prince of Wales's faction in the House of Commons. — 3, 5, 8, 18, 102[105]

STANHOPE, Charles, 3rd Earl Stanhope (1753–1815). An ardent supporter of the French Revolution; Pitt's cousin. Generally considered within the establishment to be mad, he was never prosecuted although compromised by his public statements and by his association with the SCI. — 18, 48, 95[71]

THELWALL, John (1764–1834). Political writer and lecturer; member of the Southwark Friends of the People and the LCS; member of the joint LCS/SCI Committee of Secrecy (or Correspondence). Imprisoned in the Tower and one of thirteen prosecuted for high treason in 1794. Though initially converted by Horne Tooke to the reformist cause, he declined Horne Tooke's offer to pay for him to study at Cambridge. Whether for this reason or because his uncompromising and rather bombastic public rhetoric made him too dangerous to associate with, JHT seems to have broken with him. Eventually silenced by the repressive legislation of 1795, he became for a while a successful teacher of elocution specializing in the treatment of stammering. — 8, 9, 10, 13, 17, 18, 53, 54, 70

TOOKE, William (?1720–1802). Horne Tooke's patron, whose name John Horne added to his own in 1782. JHT's book, *The Diversions of Purley*, purports to be a conversation which takes place at William Tooke's estate at

Purley, with Tooke as one of the interlocutors in Part I, along with JHT's life-long friend, Richard Beadon.

William Tooke (of Serjeant's Inn, Fleet Street) was an early treasurer, in 1769, to the Society for the Support the Bill of Rights, an association dedicated to the financial support of John Wilkes. His politics possibly stemmed from his financial connections with Alderman Thomas Oliver (brother-in-law of Alderman Richard Oliver and foundation treasurer of the Society for the Support of the Bill of Rights), with whom he had shares in the Diamond Estate in Grenada. His friendship with Horne Tooke is supposed to have been cemented by Horne Tooke's clever manoeuvres in protecting Tooke's title to his property at Purley from an enclosure bill (See Philip C. Yorke (ed.), *The Diary of John Baker* (London, 1931), p. 215).

In later life Tooke seems to have become unstable and he quarrelled with Horne Tooke, whom he had made one of his heirs. For more details of Tooke's life see Alexander Stephens, op. cit. (s. n. Baxter), II, p. 264. After his death JHT was involved in some unseemly litigation over deals supposedly struck, before Tooke's death, about the division of the estate between Horne Tooke and Tooke's nephew Captain Harwood (with whom Tooke had also quarrelled). — 18, 38, 73, 76

VAUGHAN, Felix (?1766–99). Barrister and one-time member of the LCS. Admitted to Inner Temple 1784/85. Called to the bar in November 1792. In 1797 he is listed as counsel in John Browne, *Browne's General Law List, . . . ,* 16th edn. (London, 1797), 'of Lincoln's inn — New square. Northern circuit, & West-riding of Yorksh., and Manchester–sessions'. As a member of the LCS and delegate of his division, he was the author of the *Address of the London Corresponding Society, to the other Societies of Great Britain* (London, 1792), and had travelled in revolutionary France (1790–92) writing constantly to John Richter (PRO TS 11/951/3494/1). He was junior counsel in 1794 at the trials of Hardy, Horne Tooke, and Thelwall.

During the Privy Council's re-examination of Hardy on 27 May 1794, an attempt was clearly made to implicate Vaughan in the 'treasonable practices' of the LCS. According to Hardy, however, Felix Vaughan had left the LCS twelve months previously (PRO PC 2/140 fos. 227–28, printed pagination 116–17).

He assisted at many of the political trials of the period, including those of Thomas Walker in April 1794 and of John Binns in August 1797. Vaughan died in 1799 at the early age of thirty-two. He was a wealthy man with property, bequeathing a legacy to the wife and children of the Manchester reformer Thomas Walker (see Walker, below), but leaving much of his estate to John Horne Tooke, including the proceeds of the sale of the living of 'Graffham in the County of Huntington', a property acquired by Horne Tooke during his temporary stay at Whitton in Huntingdonshire as agent for Sir Robert Bernard in the 1780s but subsequently acquired by Vaughan, who had lent him money

against it. According to Dr. Parr, Vaughan's one-time teacher (and, incident-
ally, the eventual incumbent of the living of Graffham), the relationship
between the two men was one of 'blood' (in Judith Ann Hone, *For the Cause
of Truth: radicalism in London 1796–1821* (Oxford, 1982), pp. 14–15); and other
casual references in the period refer to Vaughan as Horne Tooke's nephew.
Vaughan's own testament before the Privy Council on 5 June 1794, that he
considered Horne Tooke 'from his constant and early care and affection' as a
father (PRO PC 2/140 fo. 311, printed pagination 158), supports this view.

In a eulogistic obituary in *The Gentleman's Magazine* it transpires that he
suffered much illness, but for which

he promised fair to attain, in a few years, a conspicuous station in the foremost rank of
his profession. . . . As a forensic speaker he had scarcely any equal and but one superior
[probably Erskine]. For logical acuteness, energy of conception, and perspicuity of
arrangement, he was unrivalled. . . . When he reasoned, he convinced every mind . . .

The author concluded that, to the last hour of his existence,

he will be proud of having been honoured with his friendship; and he can never cease to
lament that a man in whom so many excellencies were united, should have been so pre-
maturely snatched from that society to which he was so bright an ornament.

The Gentleman's Magazine, 69 (1799), 358
— 5, 18, 34, 35, 36, 37, 38, 39, 40, 43, 44, 50, 72, 76, 78, 93[57], 93[59], 98[88]

WARDLE, Thomas (no dates available). Member of the SCI; member of the
joint LCS/SCI Committee of Secrecy (or Correspondence); he was indicted for
high treason in 1794 but he evaded detention. — 9, 10, 17

WHITE, Joseph (no dates available). Solicitor to the treasury. He apparently
made considerable gains by the wave of prosecutions in 1793–94. See, on his
wicked ways, Thomas Holcroft, *A Narrative of Facts, relating to a Prosecution
for High Treason* (London, 1795), p. 40. — 2, 75, 101[99]

WILKES, John (1725–97). Horne Tooke's old political associate of the 1760s,
with whom he subsequently and very publicly fell out in 1771 over the use of
funds of the Society for the Support of the Bill of Rights, which Horne Tooke
and his partisans claimed were being used on behalf of Wilkes's private inter-
ests. JHT at this time had become the *bête noire* of the Wilkite radicals and his
effigy was burned in the streets of London (Alexander Stephens, op. cit. (s. n.
Baxter), I, p. 196). — 19, 64, 105[123]